Church Planting with Paul

7 Ancient Concepts, 7 Successful Marketing Techniques to Use for Church Planting Today

Larry Waltman

iUniverse, Inc.
New York   Bloomington

Church Planting with Paul
7 Ancient Concepts, 7 Successful Marketing
Techniques to Use for Church Planting Today

iUniverse books may be ordered through booksellers or by contacting:

iUniverse
1663 Liberty Drive
Bloomington, IN 47403
www.iuniverse.com
1-800-Authors (1-800-288-4677)

Because of the dynamic nature of the Internet, any Web addresses or links contained in this book may have changed since publication and may no longer be valid.

ISBN: 978-1-4401-9192-3 (sc)
ISBN: 978-1-4401-9193-0 (ebk)

Printed in the United States of America

iUniverse rev. date: 4/23/2010

Contents

Bibliography

Crosson, John Dominic and Reed, Jonathan L., In Search of Paul: How Jesus' Apostle Opposed Rome's Empire with God's Kingdom, New York, HarperSanFrancisco, 2004

Griffith-Jones, Robin, The Gospel According to Paul, The Creative Genius Who Brought Jesus to the World, New York, HarperSanFrancisco, 2004

McManus, Barbara F., Roman Social Class and Public Display, the College of New Rochelle, July 2003, http://www.vroma.org/~bmcmanus/socialclass.html, 4 Feb 2006

Meeks, Wayne A., The First Urban Christians: The Social World of the Apostle Paul, New Haven, Yale University Press, 1983

Stark, Rodney, The Rise of Christianity: How the Obscure, Marginal Jesus Movement Became the Dominant Religious Force in the Western World in a Few Centuries, San Francisco, HarperCollins, 1997

White, L. Michael, From Jesus to Christianity, New York, Harper Collins, 2004

Biblical passages: http://biblegateway.com/cgi-bin/bible?passage=ACTS+15&version=NIV&language, July 17, 2003

All biblical quotations are taken from the New International Version (NIV) Bible

Concept of a Religious Economy

Rodney Stark introduces the concept of a "religious economy" in his 1996 book, _"The Rise of Christianity: How the Obscure, Marginal Jesus Movement Became the Dominant Religious Force in the Western World in a Few Centuries._ Stark writes:

"A _religious economy_ consists of all the religious activity going on in any society. Religious economies are like commercial economies in that they consist of a market of current and potential customers, a set of _religious firms_ seeking to serve that market, and the religious 'product lines' offered by the various firms.

The use of market language to discuss things often thought to be sacred was not, and is not, meant to offend, but to enable me to import some basic insights from economics to help explain religious phenomena..." _[Stark, p. 194]_

Stark believes that economic terms of behavior apply to religious firms. These firms can conduct market research to learn how best to introduce a "product line" or faith to potential consumers or converts. Religious firms can select target markets and develop promotional techniques to present the faith at a price a consumer is willing to pay. The faith passes on to the convert when the convert agrees to the price. In a religious economy, Paul's missionary journeys are recognizable in terms of modern strategic marketing systems.

The capacity of a single religious faith to monopolize a religious economy depends on the degree to which the government uses coercive forces to regulate the religious faiths. Stark writes, "...to the degree that a religious economy is unregulated, it will tend to be very pluralistic." _[Stark p. 194]_ The greater the number of practicing faiths there are in a defined market increases the difficulties of introducing a new faith.

Faced with a bewildering selection of faiths, myths and cults, Gentiles of the First Century were overwhelmed and unwilling, or unable, to commit totally to one single brand of religion. The variety of religious faiths made for little reliance on any one brand. People shopped from one to another.

PAUL

Into the crowded marketplace of the religious economy came Paul with a new faith known as the "The Way." At first, it was a cult of Judaism. Considering all the other religions clamoring for converts, Paul had to clearly define the unique attributes and benefits of his faith for the consumer. He had to show the rationalization that a believer accepts to make a total commitment to God. God then promises to care for the believer in this world and after death. The concept that God will care for the believer was a new and unique idea in Greco-Roman religions.

Paul believed he was under the direction of God as revealed to him in the desert after his conversion. He had the attributes, knowledge and skills to be the person most capable of carrying out God's direction for introducing the faith of The Way to the Gentiles.

Paul planned and organized missionary journeys for spreading The Way. What is unusual is that today we would consider it a marketing campaign to carry the faith of The Way beyond Judea and Galilee. Paul had unique qualities that met the criteria for success in such a campaign. He was born and raised as a Jew in the city of Tarsus in the province of Cilicia. He was a second-generation Roman citizen. He spoke Greek as his native tongue without the Jewish accent of leaders of the movement from Judea and Galilee. He was fully aware of Greco-Roman culture, customs, education, amusements, commerce and laws. During approximately 35-37 CE, Barnabas found Paul in Tarsus and convinced him to come to Antioch to work in the movement of The Way.

As a professional tent maker, he provided a critical commodity to the "defense industry" represented by the Roman Army. While civilians also used tents, the Army required massive numbers of both new and replacement tents. The Army was most often in the field, away from the garrison, policing the provinces and performing the critical design and construction of roads and aqueducts. Paul continued his skill of tent-making while on his mission, providing for his own needs so as not to be a burden to The Movement.

Despite the prosperity of his tent-making in Tarsus, Paul left it and followed Barnabas to Antioch to work in the church. Their relationship was one of patronage that was universal throughout the Empire. Barnabas was the patron, and Paul was the client.

MACROENVIRONMENTAL FORCES FOR PAUL TO NEGOTIATE

In the First Century, there were broad, commonly acknowledged forces that shaped the activities and practices for both profit and non-profit marketing, just as there are today. These environmental forces which lay outside the control of the marketing manager are called **macroenvironmental forces.** These forces include the physical environment, sociocultural institutions, demographic forces, scientific and technical knowledge, economic and competitive forces, and political and legal forces. They are always present, and a marketing manager must evaluate and contend with them. The following were macroenvironmental factors in the Greco-Roman world that Paul confronted.

The first factor was the *physical environment*, which consists of the natural world, including both animal and mineral resources. A land with domesticated and harmless animals and cultivated fields provides a different environment than one with wild and dangerous animals and deserts or forests. Climate is also a part of this environment. In a hot Mediterranean climate where citizens spend most of their time outdoors in the streets and public areas, it is easy to address them publicly.

The four months of winter in the Mediterranean created adverse sailing conditions, as well hardships for land travel. After separating from Barnabas, Paul did not leave on his first missionary trip until spring when the snow had melted in the mountain passes to the north and east of Antioch. Additionally, predatory animals and illness were always environmental hurdles in the First Century.

Social and cultural values represented the second factor. These values are expressed through abstract concepts regarding what is good or bad, right or wrong, and appropriate vs. inappropriate conduct for individuals in society. These values are part of social institutions; they are learned values, beliefs and behaviors of people. They are the mechanisms by which individuals learn to conform to society. In the First Century, Greek language and culture dominated the eastern part of the empire where Paul worked. Volunteer social associations benefitting tradesmen and guilds and crafts, as well as burial societies that ensured a "proper" funeral for members, were extremely important.

Life was lived based on who you knew and who could assist you, which reflected the rigid stratification of society. Throughout the empire, everyone had a place in society from which they rarely moved. Progressing upward through the strata was difficult, but not impossible. However, it was literally impossible to break into the imperial aristocracy of the emperor and his family, senators and their families, or the *equite* – knights and their families who represented the minor aristocracy earned through service to the state. Everyone accepted the value of pride achieved through successful accomplishments; a work ethic, pride in city and state, individual responsibility and self-fulfillment were important, and they were factors accepted by everyone.

The third factor was **demographics**: characteristics of the human population and population segments, especially when identifying consumer markets. Race, nation of origin, religion, and education level were all used to identify and sort individuals. It is important to note that there are long-established Jewish congregations in the cities Paul visited, some even from the time of the Diaspora which began in the 8th to 6th centuries BCE. While the Jews were always the minority among the Gentiles, there was a subset minority within the Gentiles which identified with the Jewish belief of monotheism. Known as God-fearers or God fearing, these Gentiles worshipped along with the Jews in their synagogues. When Paul was rejected by the Jews, it was the Gentile God-fearers that he chose to target.

There was a constant migration of free men, foreigners and slaves through the empire. Famine, illness, and destruction caused by floods, earthquakes and fires forced them to continually search for a better life. Massive numbers of new slaves from newly conquered peoples or state-sponsored enslavements also moved around the empire. An example of state enslavement is the 14,000 male Jewish slaves taken to Rome after the destruction of the Second Temple in 70 CE. The slaves were transported with the gold, silver, and precious gems taken from the Temple. The Romans used the booty from the Temple in Jerusalem to finance the Coliseum and used the Jewish slaves to build the Coliseum.

Science and technology, a fourth factor, was vastly different from what we think of as science and technology today, but it was just as important then as it is now. Science is the gathering of knowledge about people and the environment, and technology is the application of that amassed knowledge for practical purposes. In the First Century, science was limited to the observations of physical phenomena. Greeks gathered observations of the sun, moon, stars and tides for hundreds of years and taught about these observations in schools.

Divination and consulting the astrological signs, as reported in the Journey of the Magi, Matthew 2:2-12, was normal for the times. Divination also included reading the signs of flights of birds and entrails of sacrificed animals. Science and superstition went hand in hand as a key part of the imperial religion that Augustus was responsible for reviving. The fact that there were germs that could cause illness was unknown, and it was impossible to predict droughts, famines, or plagues.

"Paul was moving about in a world where absurd superstitions were swallowed wholesale. Some of his own ideas, which would strike a modern as extraordinary – his belief in demons and spirits and his view that human beings could be conveyed from one spiritual 'dimension' to another, rather like a traveler in outer space – would have been perfectly intelligible to his contemporaries.... In the world of classical antiquity, however, most people would have accepted the powers of the unseen; it was simply a question of which demons or gods were better than another, or, if you were Jewish, which were legitimate. One of the reasons for the Jewish religion being so popular was the widely held belief that Jews were good fortune tellers...The point at issue in Philippi *[when Paul cast out the demons from the slave girl fortune-telling [reported in Acts 16:16-19]* is not the lawfulness of fortune-telling, still less its efficacy, but who was in charge. Paul was regarded as a threat by the astrologers because he was a threat; he was deliberately posing one. A new commodity had arrived, which Paul was selling hard, and if it took hold and became popular, it would inevitably drive the rival spiritual attractions out of business." *[Wilson p. 147]*

Technological advances were limited mainly to construction and civil engineering. The Romans developed the arch to support massive weight. Civil engineering enabled aqueduct builders to run water troughs and sluices with settlement basins for miles across open land and through rivers and mountains. A steady gradient of 1/200th of an inch over land and through rivers and mountains kept the water flowing. The aqueduct for the city of Caesarea Maritima in Judea – which still stands in ruins – brought water from ten miles away. The discovery of waterproof cement led to the construction of harbors where needed. At Caesarea Maritima, engineers built Herod's Harbor with the waterproof cement technique and enclosed three acres for safe anchorage [www.bibleplaces.com/caesarea.html, Jan. 9, 2007]. However, they did not develop a technique to build curves into a road; Roman roads ran straight, using right angles to change directions.

Economic and competitive factors are a strong influence in any economy; this held true in a religious economy. An economic system shows how a society will allocate resources for goods and services. In the religious economic system, individuals elected how to spend their physical and spiritual time. Competitive factors consist of four basic types of market structure: pure competition, monopolistic competition, oligopoly, and monopoly.

Pure competition in a religious economy is free entry of any faith, with many faiths for many consumers. The religious market had many small firms competing with each other for many buyers. Buyers or sellers did not control prices. There was a steady supply of faiths and a steady demand for the faiths. Rome did not apply any constrictions on religions and purposely allowed peoples and cultures to retain their religions and practices – as long as they also worshiped or paid homage to the Emperor. Jews were persecuted by the state because they refused to honor the Imperial Religion.

Monopolistic competition in a religious economy consists of a large number of faiths offering similar products with slightly differentiated identities and prices. In a religious economy, there are a large number of separate religions offering similar faiths, worship practices, care of the worshiper by the god, and a variety of eschatological answers. (*Eschatology* is any system of doctrines concerning last or final matters, or death, the judgment, the future state, etc.). Religious organizations exerted control over the price one had to pay to become a member of a particular religion or sect. Greco-Roman religions in the First Century were in monopolistic competition, offering similar products for the worshiper in this lifetime, and eschatological systems after death. Because of the differences in the variety of religious wares and articles, a religion could control the cost for the individual to join the particular faith by claiming better benefits and usefulness for the member.

Oligopoly competition is a market structure where a small number of sellers dominate the market, such as two or three faiths.

Monopoly competition is a market with only one product or brand, and there are no substitutes. The Roman Catholic Church exerted monopolistic competition and dominated Western Europe from the collapse of the Roman Empire to the Reformation.

Political and legal forces were additional factors in the macroenvironment, consisting of the structure and practices of the government and the legal environment of laws and regulations, along with their interpretation as applied to society and to the religious firms. An example is one single faith controlling the politics of the community, and that faith induces lawmakers to pass laws that the faith desires. Political and legal forces combine when the controlling faith makes it unlawful for missionaries of another faith to come into the territory, such as what happened in Ephesus.

All of these macroenvironmental factors that have just been listed can change over long periods. Paul structured his missionary campaign with knowledge of the macroenvironmental restrictions of the peoples, the culture, the physical environments, and the political world. While the person leading the missionary journey does not control the macroenvironmental forces, the leader of the missionary journey does react to them. They are occurring naturally all around and are dominant. Unless the leader of the missionary effort can turn facts and forces to his advantage, he will be unsuccessful in his campaign.

MICROENVIRONMENTAL FORCES & THE FOUR C's OF MARKETING

The function of marketing also deals with four microenvironmental elements that are controllable: *Company, Customer, Competition and Collaborator.* The marketing director controls these four factors which influence every marketing campaign. They are variable elements that the marketing director uses to combat the macroenvironmental forces in any campaign.

The *company* is the first of these microenvironmental forces. A company is a functioning organization that offers services to consumers. In Paul's case, the company conveyed or offered the faith of the Jesus Movement to others. Barnabas and Paul, along with the elders of the Jesus Movement in Antioch, were a new, or "start up," company. While Acts does not list in detail the planning for the first campaign or missionary journey, it does address how money was raised for the trip. Barnabas and Paul knew all the doubts, worries, setbacks and disappointments of a startup venture, along with the elation, pride of accomplishment and self-actualization that comes with success. The first short journey, perhaps not well planned and undoubtedly unsuccessful, was full of danger. After the two returned to Antioch, Paul knew that any additional campaigns must involve serious and thorough planning.

Paul was an entrepreneur – a risk-taker, not a risk-avoider. Because of the directions God revealed to him in the desert after his conversion, Paul believed his mission in life was to carry the faith to the Jews. He knew he could not let the opportunity pass. Paul fiercely believed the faith he received directly from God in the desert was the only true faith and doctrine and that anything else was in error. He saw himself as a special agent and envoy of God, called to undertake the task of introducing The Way of the Jesus Movement to Jews, and more especially the Gentile God-fearers.

"Paul viewed himself as a special agent called by God to perform a certain task. That task, in keeping with the language of Isaiah and Jeremiah, was to serve as a prophet, or 'light,' to the nations… there is no sense that he had left Judaism behind either by becoming a follower of the Jesus Movement or in his reaching out to non-Jews…many scholars prefer to define Paul's experience as a 'calling' rather than a conversion'… Paul had not 'converted' away from Judaism. Rather, he had merely 'converted' from one sect of Judaism, the Pharisee, to another, while staying within the same worldview and set of values." *[White p.157]*

The Council of Jerusalem was an entrepreneurial organization that encouraged individuals to take risks and gave them the autonomy to develop new programs as needed. The Council consisted of elders and apostles of the movement in Jerusalem who knew Jesus personally; Acts considers the Council the authority of the Movement. The Council encouraged Paul and the elders in Antioch to take risks to convey the faith to others. The Council also gave him the opportunity to preach the creed as he saw fit. The Council, like Paul, believed itself to be Jewish but to represent a new apocalyptic cult within Judaism.

The second element in the microenvironment is the **customer.** A company that does not satisfy the customer does not last long. The customers in a religious economy are converts. The customer has more influence on a company than anything else. The needs of the customer must be satisfied for the company to remain in business. The company may believe it is fulfilling the customer's wants and needs. The only element to determine what the customer wants is the customer. The need of the customer is "economic utility." The company must fulfill the economic utility by goods or services that fulfill the customer's real or perceived wants and needs. Within economic utility are four core concerns: *form utility*, *place utility*, *time utility* and *possession utility*.

Form utility involves placing the beliefs into a form the convert can and will use. Remembering the body and blood of Christ is form utility in the communion service. The use of the communion service is a form that the convert can and will use.

Place utility involves passing on the belief wherever a potential convert wants to hear it. Place utility insures the ready convert can hear the belief beside a river, in an earthquake-damaged jail, or in a city square.

Time utility involves passing on the belief whenever a potential convert wants to hear it. This can be on a Sabbath morning, or in the middle of the night after an earthquake.

Possession utility means passing on the belief in a meaningful manner for the convert to feel ownership of the belief. Possession utility occurs through baptism for the convert. This ritual or rite symbolizes the acquiring and possession of the faith for the convert. Through baptism, the convert is "born anew" and possesses the belief and faith.

The third element of the microenvironment is *competition*. Rival religions or beliefs compete for converts in the same market. A major task for the manager is to identify and understand the competition and set his product apart from all others. To do this, the director analyzes *product class, product category* and *brand*. He uses these three definitions or categories to identify products.

The term *product class* refers to a broad group of commodities or beliefs that differ somewhat but perform similar functions or benefits. The *product category* is a subset of product class containing only beliefs of a certain type, such as a liberal interpretation or fundamental interpretation of the belief. The *brand* is an identifying feature that isolates various denominations from all others in the class. The brand is the specific set of beliefs.

There are four types of competition: price, quality, time and location.

Price competition determines that for a convert to obtain the benefits of the belief, he or she must pay a certain price or prices. Such price to the convert could be persecution, suffering, or even death, which makes the success of The Way all the more remarkable. All of the accoutrements and effects of the product, other than price, remain the same.

A second type is quality competition. This is more complicated than price competition because converts define quality in many ways. Durability, reliability, fellowship, and prompt, polite and friendly service are attributes of quality the customer places on the belief. The definitions of quality may be high, but the convert is willing to pay a high price for a belief that satisfies him or her. Quality competition in religions is the reliability of the beliefs in the convert's mind.

A third type is time competition, in that the belief is available at the time it is wanted. It is the ability to deliver the goods or services when the consumer needs them. Examples are Lydia's conversion, and the midnight earthquake at the jail. *[Acts 16:11-34]*

Location competition, the forth factor, is emphasized in the real estate mantra, "Location, Location, and Location." The manager wants to use the best place to meet prospective converts. Paul perhaps looked for temples or cult centers where he could find people thinking about their beliefs. Other locations could be outside a theater, a bath, or athletic facility – anywhere he could reach an audience as he talked. The city squares with water fountains were good sites because most of an individual's time was spent outside the apartment, and everyone came to the public fountains to get water.

Collaborators are the fourth element in the microenvironment. A collaborator is a person or company, not a member of the marketing organization, who helps the organization do its business. Some are specialists who provide special services or production equipment. Suppliers are collaborators that provide materials and equipment. Terms like *alliances, networks,* or *informal partnerships* apply to collaborators. Gospel bookstores in various towns or souvenir shops at large churches are collaborators in our contemporary culture.

THE 4 P'S OF MARKETING

In the largest sense, a market is where buyers and sellers come together. It is a group of potential converts who may want to adopt the belief after exposure to it. These potential converts have an interest in accepting the belief system and have the ability and willingness to pay an established price. The market is where there is an exchange of a value by a buyer and a seller. In the marketplace of a religious economy, the market is where the faith is passed on to the convert in exchange for something of value: the promise to support and live by the tenets of the belief. A ritual act of the transfer in the baptism signifies the exchange of the faith for the promise to live in accordance with the faith. A marketing campaign today seeks to influence potential converts to accept the faith as presented to them.

The point of exchange is not the end of the process. It costs the marketing agency much more to find a new believer than to maintain a believer. Maintaining a believer over the long run is *relationship marketing*. This is the idea that the converted believer will stay with the faith. Paul practiced relationship marketing in his letters to the churches and during his return visits to the churches, along with the visits of Silas, Timothy and Titus.

There are four separate components, each under the control of the manager, which can help in acquiring the maximum number of consumers or converts. Planning and carrying out a successful marketing campaign involves blending these separate tasks. Taken together they are the "marketing mix." The marketing manager mixes, matches, and combines these components in differing quantities and combinations to gain the greatest response from the target market. These separate components are known as *product*, *place* (or distribution), *promotion*, and *price*.

A *product* can be goods, services or beliefs that offer a bundle of tangible and intangible attributes to satisfy a convert. Converts expect more than a single tangible or intangible core product from taking on the new belief of the Jesus Movement. These additional attributes are the total product or total belief. A marketing manager should be certain that the convert knows about and is aware of the total product. For example, the core product of a commercial airline is to move passengers and cargo from one point to another. The extras include courteous service, clean and comfortable facilities, on-time departure and arrivals, etc.

The core product of The Way, or the Jesus Movement, is salvation and eternal life through Jesus Christ and the presence and power of the Holy Spirit. It is victory over death. In the imperial religion of the empire, the core product was victory over opponents, providing peace for the empire. Belonging to the Jesus Movement provided a package of additional benefits or extras for the believer. Membership in a house-church was a substitute for the professional associations and burial societies so important and necessary in the society. Membership provided the possibility of forming patron and client relationships. And the membership provided an extended family for orphans and widows. The first church in Corinth formed around Aquila, who was a tent maker. Initial members were conceivably professional tent makers and personal acquaintances of Aquila. They knew each other on a professional as well as personal level.

An additional benefit of the Jesus Movement was the command to love one another. Life in the first century was harsh and often lonely. Death was ever-present from spoiled foods to illnesses with no known cures. The emphasis of the church on acts of mercy and the doctrine to love other believers and non-believers was a much-welcomed additional benefit in the bitter everyday world where death and destruction was rampant.

The urban population of the day was mobile, and people were often driven to new cities by famine, plagues or destruction of living spaces. This new religion, with a house-church that cared for believers as if they were family, provided a much-needed anchor. The community of believers also provided nursing assistance, companionship and funerals. Believers could abandon the almost universal and expensive burial societies. These societies collected money from members as burial insurance to guarantee the members received a "proper funeral," the final act that was so important in Roman society.

The house-churches also enhanced the universal and omnipresent patron-client relationships. Lydia was a wealthy woman from Thyatira who marketed the incredibly expensive purple cloth used for imperial robes and a trim for senators' togas. She became Paul's patron by inviting him to stay in her house. She could be the patron of the church in Thyatira [Acts 16:11-16]. Phoebe, a deacon of the church in the upscale Corinthian suburb of Cenchrea on the eastern side of the Ismuth, was a patron to Paul and the house-church in Cenchrea. Her personal wealth enabled her to take Paul's letter to the Romans.

Place, or distribution, is the second component of the four P's of marketing. This part of the marketing mix involves all actions that go into placing the services or beliefs before a consumer or convert at the best location and at a right time to "make a sale." Place involves four factors: *manufacturer, wholesaler, retailer,* and *the ultimate customer.*

The *manufacturer* is the organization that recognizes a consumer has needs or wants and provides a product, service or belief to satisfy the need. Paul and the church in Antioch believed Jews had a need to hear the Jesus message.

The Antioch church was the *wholesaler,* or home office, of the campaign. Paul and his companions were the retail element in this mix, dealing directly with the potential convert. They went out to the various cities and met one-on-one with potential converts. They passed on the belief to interested converts, making them believers. After the core group of believers formed in a city, they became the retail element, telling their friends and others about the belief. Paul and his companions were the first *retailers* in a city. The first converts then became the retailers, passing on the faith so Paul could move on.

The *ultimate consumer* was the individual new believer in the Movement. This ultimate consumer accepted and internalized the belief and practices of the Jesus Movement along with all the enhancements, including the basic belief that Jesus is the awaited Redeemer. Additional benefits included companionship in the worship service and meal, love and concern for each other, and acts of mercy for others; all were attributes of the belief.

Promotion is the third component of the 4 P's of marketing. It includes all forms of marketing communications. The first century was a culture free from media tricks. However, in the first century the best form of promotion, as it is today, was hearing about a belief from a recognizable person whose opinion was valued. The promotion efforts provided information about the faith and instructions regarding the practices of the faith to new local converts. One new convert would accept the faith directly from Paul and then would tell friends and others about his new faith. The original convert was seen as a trusted source in the mind of the second-level convert. Learning from someone you know and trust was the best promotion then, as it is now. "Word of mouth" ranks highest in credibility of all means of promotion. A testimonial is especially persuasive if it comes from a trusted source.

Organizations promote a product or faith in a format that marketing managers believe will have a positive impact on a targeted audience or potential convert. In the first century, public preaching and teaching was effective. Today's promotions target specific genders, ages, races, education levels, incomes, etc. Baranabas and Paul targeted Jews on their first short campaign. But they soon learned, by the hostility of the synagogue leaders, that the most fertile audience was the Gentile God-fearer who believed in the god of the Jews. This person was usually the head of a household. When the head of the household converted, the rest of the household, including slaves, relatives and clients, also converted and accepted the new belief. The promotions always aimed at city dwellers because in first century society, those who lived outside the city were without influence.

Another form of promotion was the miracle, a necessary requirement of all religions in the first century in order to provide credibility. If your god could not cause or execute something supernatural, then how valid could this alleged god be? Paul performed miracles without touching the person. In Philippi, a slave girl who told everyone that Paul and his companions were servants of the Most High God followed him. Paul became so troubled he turned and commanded a spirit to "come out of her." *[Acts 16:16-18]* At another time in Ephesus, Acts reports: "God did extraordinary miracles through Paul, so that even handkerchiefs and aprons that had touched him were taken to the sick, and their illnesses were cured and the evil spirits left them." *[Acts 19:11-12]*

Price is the fourth component of the 4 P's of marketing. Price is an amount of money, or consideration of something of value, given in order to receive a product, creed or faith. The seller determined what perceived value a potential convert places on the belief he or she will receive. The Jerusalem Council spent considerable time in coming to a price one would pay in order to join The Way.

Traditional circumcised Jews from Judea and Galilee made up the membership of the Jesus Movement cult of Judaism. These who were originally Jews and now were members of the Jesus Movement demanded a Gentile believer undergo the rite of circumcision. Paul saw it as an unnecessary and extremely harsh price for an adult to pay. The price must be something of value to the buyer but cannot exceed what the buyer can reasonably consider to pay.

Arguments over the cost of membership in The Movement went on from 46 to 51 CE while Paul and Barnabas were in Antioch after the first missionary journey. Finally, the elders of the Antioch church sent Paul and Barnabas to Jerusalem to place the question before the Jerusalem Council, the supreme authority for The Movement. The Council held a long discussion over what the price should be for Gentiles to become members of The Movement. Many members spoke, including the Disciple Peter. Finally, James, the brother of Jesus and leader of the Council, announced the Council's findings. They including abstaining from food sacrificed to idols, from blood, from meat of strangled animals, and from sexual immorality. The dietary laws were understandable because they are part of the Jewish kosher dietary rules. There was no further explanation on the rule to abstain from sexual immorality. There is no indication if the Council meant to follow the strict and prudent laws of Moses, if it meant to prevent debauchery and unwholesome relations with male and female temple prostitutes of pagan gods, or to prevent sexual relations with close members of the immediate family. Because the Greeks celebrate the pleasures of the body, their interpretation of sexual morals was less strict compared to the Jews.

Price is always subject to change in the economy. It appeared the price for joining the Jesus Movement changed during Paul's long years on the campaign. They adjusted to what the consumer would pay. When Paul set off on his marketing campaign in 46, he priced the faith – as dictated by the Council of Jerusalem – at the three kosher dietary laws and the rule of sexual morality.

In 52-54 CE, Paul wrote to the Corinthians about food sacrificed to idols. He said, "We know that an idol is nothing at all in the world and that there is no God but one." *[1 Cor. 8:4]* He went on to say that food sacrificed to idols was acceptable; however, if someone saw you eating food sacrificed to an idol, he may be emboldened to eat the food, not having your knowledge that an idol is nothing.

By the spring of 56, Paul was writing his letter to the Romans. In this, the last letter, he did not mention the three kosher dietary laws. In fact, he wrote, "As one who is in the Lord Jesus, I am fully convinced that no food is unclean in itself. But if anyone regards something as unclean, then for him it is unclean. If your brother is distressed because of what you eat, you are no longer acting in love." *[Rom. 14:14-15]* He did mention to the Romans many acts of "wickedness, evil, greed and depravity" and specifically condemned and denounced lesbian and homosexual acts. *[Rom. 1:26-32]*

The marketing mix was what Paul made of it. He had to combine the *product* with the *place*, add in the promotion, and finally set the *price*. He emphasized the quality of the product in some cities; in others, he emphasized place, as he did in Philippi when administering to Lydia and to the jail governor. And at some other place, at another time, he may have de-emphasized price. What the combination would be depended on the genius of Paul's marketing skills at any given time.

Step 1

Look for Opportunities for Success

You can learn how to establish a new church or plant new Christian communities using the same successful techniques the Apostle Paul used in the first century. Paul took God's instruction "to do the work he was given to do" and initiated a seven-step program to spread the new faith, the Jesus Movement, from Antioch in Syria to Corinth in Greece.

This is a book that shows you Paul's successful techniques for spreading the faith, planting new churches and establishing new Christian communities in what was a very crowded religious economy with well-established and well-funded competition for converts and believers. Together we will look at each of Paul's steps, see what he did, and then apply that to your quest to plant a church or establish a Christian faith community.

Let's first remember Paul failed in his first attempt to plant churches and establish new faith communities. The old adage, "haste makes waste," possibly applies here. Paul and Barnabas were so enthused with the message of the Holy Spirit in Acts 13:21 that they set off to spread their faith with seemingly little or no planning. Consequently, as you well know, that first abbreviated missionary journey had no end of failures at every turn.

We can learn from Paul's mistakes as well as from his successes. We discuss the seven steps of his program, which includes four planning stages, one executing stage, and one controlling and evaluating stage. For the final stage, we'll discuss Paul's planning of a bigger and better campaign to Spain.

When you start to think about how to plant a church, you need to start thinking about it from the values and positions of *non-churchgoers*. What are the values and needs of those who have no church? Why don't they have a church or faith group? In other words, you are planning the founding of a church or faith group from outside of the church or faith group. You will look at your church, which is your product, and see where you can satisfy the individual wants and needs of the non-churchgoers, particularly what will motivate them to join your church.

Are there values and practices in your church or Christian community that address the values, wants and needs of the non-churchgoers? Paul made the mistake on his first missionary journey of focusing on the churchgoers, or synagogue-going Jews. He was not able to penetrate that market.

The first step is to look for opportunities for success. There is no sense butting your head against a wall for converts if there is no opportunity for success. Paul certainly thought there were opportunities for success as he and Barnabas went off to Cyprus. They were responding to the Holy Spirit's speaking to the leaders of the Antioch Church saying "Set apart for me Baranabas and Paul for the work to which I have called them." *[Acts 13:21]* There is, however, no indication in Acts that Paul did any research on what the synagogue Jews on Cyprus thought about, or how to go about bringing them into the new Jesus Movement faith. Barnabas and Paul possibly believed the Holy Spirit would open all doors and lay everything out for them.

How could Paul have looked for opportunities for success? Just how can you look for opportunities for success today? The first thing to do is to make a **situational analysis.** That's the term for making an interpretation or researching the characteristics of the environment where you plan to go and considering your organization's ability to take advantage of possible opportunities. Making a situational analysis involves *environmental scanning,* which is evaluating the macroenvironment separate and apart from your organization. It is the environment over which you have no control. At this point you are looking for what the non-churchgoers are doing. What are their activities and lifestyles? Are people settled and content? What is the rate of unemployment? What is the level of education, and what is the quality of the public schools? Are there a number of minorities in the community? How do they get along? Are there a significant number of families or individuals disabled, on food stamps, or in the WIC program? What is the state of healthcare and are there many on Medicaid? Are there many stable extended families? Are there many single parent families? What is the size of the homeless community? Why haven't the non-churchgoers joined any established churches or faith communities?

Does the government allow new faith-based communities and churches? Will you need licenses? Will you have to buy permits for meetings and events you plan to hold? How many other faiths or beliefs are trying to set up programs in the community? Like Paul, you need answers for questions like these.

Stopping at every synagogue on Cyprus failed to develop any converts. The follow-up visits to synagogues at Antioch in Pisidian, Iconium and Lystra were also unsuccessful. The trip was so ill-fated that Paul was stoned and left for dead at Lystra, the third city he visited. It was then that he and Barnabas gave up and returned home to Antioch. No Jews were converted by Paul's mission, although the Book of Acts does try to put the best face on it. Acts tells there were some God-fearing Gentiles who joined, and Paul visited them on the return route to Antioch.

You can clearly see what happened to Paul when he had no research to perform a situational analysis. And you can't afford to introduce your new church or faith community without any research. If you don't do research and environmental scanning before you go into the communities, you are at the mercy of events and activities which you cannot control – like Paul was.

Paul thought his target market was the synagogue Jew. This market segment was totally satisfied with their faith and practice and clearly didn't want to hear about any new cult. By the time Paul gave up, he had written off the synagogue Jew. If he was to have any success in spreading the Jesus Movement, he would have to ignore the Jewish communities. He then had the major and basic problem of determining his target market segment. The target market segment must be receptive to his message and be large enough to provide a meaningful response to any campaign.

Another part of a situational analysis is internal to your organization. It is an evaluation of your own microenvironment that you can respond to, control and change when necessary. Here you are looking for strengths, weaknesses, opportunities and threats (SWOT). Just what are the internal strengths of your organization? What are the weaknesses? Is your strength only in your commitment, or are there additional conditions that contribute to internal strength? Make a list of your strengths, question each, and make sure you are truthful in your evaluations. Next develop a written list of weaknesses. Be sure to include any potential weaknesses, which financial and ideological supporters may leave you. Have others look at the lists of strengths and weaknesses. If you are afraid to seek help from others, you may have a major weakness in your management style – the inability to listen to objective evaluations.

In addition to the strengths and weaknesses internal to your organization, there are opportunities and threats outside the organization that you may have the ability to respond to and possibly control. Perform gaming of possible courses of action and develop responses to potential outcomes. You may be able to turn threats into opportunities. However well you think you plan, there is the chance that your target market will reject you, as happened in Paul's case. There may be no threats to your life, but existing religious groups and churches can bring law suits against you, or convince the city government to pass ordnances prohibiting you from developing your church or religious community.

Don't be blinded as Paul was in the assumption that you know everything that is out there. Your campaign is going to cost a lot of time and money, and certainly energy on your part. You are putting your whole self into the campaign. And don't think that planting a church or forming a new faith community doesn't have economic parameters. You are dealing with a religious economy that has winners and losers. Make lists of external opportunities and threats and have a third party review them. Don't be overly cautious, but be very realistic.

The differences between the internal strengths and weaknesses and external opportunities and threats is of major importance This is called the *strategic gap* and is the difference between where the organization is and where it strives to be. The success of your program depends on how you resolve that gap. Success depends on minimizing those differences between what you can control in *strengths* and *weaknesses* and what you want to control from outside *opportunities* and *threats*.

Success in planting a church or developing a new faith community depends on you taking advantage of opportunities for success. Looking back at Paul, he did not seem to have a realistic idea of whether or not there were opportunities for success for his mission. He was unable to make any changes in his plan or to take different courses of action. He and Baranabas received "a call" and couldn't wait to do the Lord's bidding. You are probably very much like them; you can't wait to get started.

They have strength in their belief, but they have a weakness they may not know about. They think all they have to do is to go into a synagogue and give a sermon which logically argues that Christ is the Redeemer. There is a sample or format sermon in Acts 13:16-41 that states that everyone was supposed to understand and join the faith Paul was advocating. Paul used an "injection" approach, whereby all he had to do was inject the convert with the facts and he would come over to the new belief Paul was extolling.

Paul's situational analysis was badly flawed. The strategic gap was greater than they had imagined, and they were unable to devise a plan during the course of the trip to resolve the vast difference. They certainly were not ready to be totally rejected by the synagogues, nor by the civic leaders the local Jews stirred up.

The lesson for Paul, and for you, is to conduct research to find opportunities for success with your product. The lack of research for Paul almost led to his death. Your lack of research probably will not lead to attacks on your life, but at the very least it will result in a colossal waste of time, talent, and money.

The good news from his first failed missionary journey, or marketing campaign, was that Paul gathered reliable and useful information indicating that Jews were not interested, but some Gentiles were. It was anecdotal based on personal observation and incidents, so it can't be considered scientific research. It can't be replicated or repeated to determine if the same findings will occur. But anecdotal research is certainly better than no research at all.

When conducting your research to find opportunities for success, you can do as Paul did: visit several cities or parts of cities where you think there will be opportunities, and evaluate what you find. You also have the internet, which provides access to many different research options, including census data, information relative to specific cities or towns, and a whole host of print and electronic information you can review free of charge. Find out what the lifestyles and values of your intended markets are. Make a preliminary evaluation to estimate what opportunities for success you will have for church planting or establishing faith communities. Save yourself from Paul's problems, which cost him effort, time, money, and nearly cost him his life.

◆ ◆ ◆

SOME QUESTIONS FOR YOU

1. How do you determine strengths in an honest manner?

2. What are some ways to understand your weaknesses?

3. How are you going to find real opportunities?

4. Are there known, as well as unknown, threats? How can you minimize unknown threats?

5. How do you go about closing a strategic gap?

6. If you are not totally certain how you can overcome strategic gap problems, where and when can you make changes to adjust internal strengths and weaknesses or external opportunities and threats?

Step 2

Find Your Market

To talk about church planting or establishing faith groups in contemporary marketing terms does nothing to diminish the process. Planting a church is introducing a new product into a market. It is comparable to introducing a new brand into the automobile market. Planting a new church in a community is introducing a new competitor into the existing mix of religions in the community. Marketing terms also give us a frame of reference in today's consumer-based world. The Spirit today moves your effort to plant a church in the religious marketplace just as the Spirit moved Paul to introduce the faith into the religious marketplaces of the cities in the Empire.

In Step 1, we discussed how Paul set out from Antioch looking for opportunities where he could successfully introduce his faith of the Jesus Movement. He believed his new faith of Jesus the Redeemer would be attractive to any Jew. He preached Jesus Christ as the Redeemer for whom the Jews had been waiting. The idea was so simple and true to Paul that he thought any Jew would understand who Jesus was. Initially Paul was not interested in approaching Gentiles with their Greek and Roman gods and their mysteries and cults practiced in the Empire. But after the sermon at Pisidian Antioch, as written in Acts 13:46, Paul and Barnabas decided they would turn to the Gentiles.

> "Then Paul and Barnabas answered them boldly: 'We had to speak the word of God to you first. Since you reject it and do not consider yourselves worthy of eternal life, we now turn to the Gentiles. For this is what the Lord has commanded us: 'I have made you a light for the Gentiles, that you may bring salvation to the ends of the earth.'" *[Acts 13:46-47]*

The faith had grown rapidly in Antioch, and Paul believed that anywhere he took The Movement, Jews would converge on the concept. You are probably like Paul. You've had a life-changing experience in acknowledging

Jesus as the Redeemer, and you believed you have been called to share your faith with non-churchgoers. You may believe that sharing your faith with others and their acceptance of it a "no-brainer;" God is with you and there is no way you can lose.

But we all know that persuading someone to accept a new idea isn't quite as simple as giving someone an "injection" of a faith or sharing an idea to which the person will immediately respond. Maybe that is the method you tried in your campaign to plant a church or build a faith community. Perhaps you sought out a town or neighborhood that appeared to you as if those living there would accept your message. Perhaps you rented a hall or a storefront, hanging a sign out that welcomed all to stop by to hear your message of the Lord. But did you first consider what the local non-churchgoers value and desire from a church? Maybe they don't feel responsive to what they have heard about your message.

Paul used the one-time injection approach on his first missionary journey. He and Barnabas were on a marketing campaign to bring their faith to Jews. They themselves were both Jews, so who better to bring new of the new faith to other Jews? It was natural because both Paul and Barnabas were Jews before they accepted Jesus. They were leaders in the Jesus Movement in Antioch, and it was there that they were called by God to do the work He set aside for them, which was to take the faith to other Jews throughout the Empire. What they found was that no market existed among the synagogue Jews living in the Empire. The preliminary target market did not respond positively to their message. Maybe you have discovered there was no response to your storefront mission. To your dismay, the non-churchgoers are not interested. To Paul's bewilderment, the synagogue Jews to whom he preached were not interested. In fact, the Jews were so insulted by his message that they had the city government throw Paul and Barnabas out of one city. A group of Jewish hotheads formed a posse and chased after them. When the posse caught up with Paul and Barnabas, they incited a riot against them. Paul was beaten badly and left for dead. In fact, throughout his many journeys, Paul was often beaten and jailed by Jews, as happened during the riot in Ephesus.

Paul and Barnabas finally realized that their idea of a market was flawed and that they were not going to make headway with synagogue Jews in cities of the Empire. Perhaps you are at a point where you've spent enough time and money attempting to attract non-churchgoers to your new church or faith based community, and you've determined that the market is not what you thought it was. So, what's the smart thing to do? Cut your losses and start again with a better plan!

A *market* is a group of potential consumers who want a product and have the resources, the willingness, and the ability to acquire it. There is also a broader *total market* consisting of all the potential consumers in a defined area or context. A total market is so huge that there will be a vast number of consumers who will have no interest in the product. Effort, time, and money are lost in trying to appeal to everyone in a total market. Messages or promotions designed to attract everyone are usually so broad that they do not get the attention of anyone.

The total market is too big. Instead, identify a *market segment* characterized by shared traits or common features among members. Design and direct messages and promotions to influence that market segment. There is no reason not to approach non-churchgoers based their common values and wants. People today, much like in the first century, will feel more comfortable with organizations that share and reflect their own values, beliefs and activities.

Dividing a large, mixed total market into segments is done by identifying the segments by shared characteristics or common features. One way to segment a market is to sort by age and/or sex. Messages designed for seniors are different from those designed for young adults. Messages targeting one sex are different from those appealing to the other sex. Additionally, marital status can influence the messages to which a targeted person listens.

A second way of grouping segments is through socioeconomic factors, which reflect an individual's social position or economic standing. Some individuals may have high-income status but work in a blue-collar profession. Others may have low-income status but hold high social positions, such as a college professor. This category is complicated, and care should be taken in developing criteria for this segment.

A worker on a shop floor who hunts and fishes for recreation has a different lifestyle from an information systems technician who may have a comparable salary, but spends time with his children and follows professional sports. Shopkeepers in the first century had different lifestyles than masons and carpenters.

Geographic segmentation is also important when grouping individuals into market segments. People who live in an upscale suburb may have different needs, values, and desires from people who live in older established sections of a city. People living on farms in Ohio may have different needs, values, and desires from people who live on farms in Kansas.

Even behavior and consumption patterns define markets. Some consumers purchase clothes only in specialty stores while others buy their clothes in discount stores. Individuals can be grouped by the benefits they seek from a product, such as what they want from their clothes. Is it style, functionality, or something else? Differing target markets for automobiles are indicated by what those individuals consider important in terms of luxury, performance, operating costs, etc.

Any and all of these factors can be used to define and rank consumers into target market segments that have one or more traits in common. You may feel you have a good chance of success with the target market of new homeowners in a new suburb. There are a number of common traits among these homeowners. They are probably young families in their 30s and 40s. The men will all have college degrees, perhaps in fields such as engineering, information technology, or other technical fields, or they may be medical technicians or nurses. They are most likely familiar with black and white issues with scientifically-defined results. The women are also likely to have college degrees and careers in a variety of fields. The families will have two or more children ranging in age from infants to middle-school age.

This target market may be looking for a religious education for their children in a Sunday school setting. They may also be interested in spiritual experiences facilitated through membership in a church or faith community. These adults may want more connections with others who are concerned Christians like themselves. They may want friends in the congregation who share their faith and practice it through home groups. They may be searching for opportunities to demonstrate their faith through community projects; perhaps they will want to go on missionary trips within the United States or even overseas.

You have gone through the process of sorting non-churchgoers into target market segments that share common traits. You can now identify a target segment and list values and practices that such individuals desire in a church or faith group.

With the market segmentation and identification completed, you now have specific ideas in mind for how to fine-tune your message to engage the target market. You can now emphasize values you believe the target market desires and will embrace. You can deliver your message through teaching and preaching in defined ways that will meet the needs of the target market segment. You can place a price on joining your church or faith group. The price should be high enough to ensure that joining will be special to the individual, but not so high that you shut out potential converts.

Paul and Barnabas returned to Antioch with research results they obtained at great expense of time, money and personal safety. The research was anecdotal and not scientific, which means it could not be replicated. However, it was better than no research at all. It clearly showed that the synagogue Jews in cities throughout the Empire were not interested and that additional campaigning to the group would be useless. They were not interested in leaving behind the religion they brought with them during the time of the Diaspora hundreds of years before.

However, a totally unforeseen market segment responded to their message. The God-fearing Gentiles, as Acts labeled them, believed in monotheism and worshiped alongside other Jews who also prayed to a monotheistic god. In the Greco-Roman lifestyle, these Gentiles were almost all men and heads of households, although there were also Greek women who ran their own businesses and held the role of head of a household. These men could not become Jews and fully enter into Jewish worship of the monotheistic god because they were uncircumcised; however, many did not want to be circumcised.

A socioeconomic evaluation would show they were comprised primarily of craftsmen, artisans, soldiers and shopkeepers. They were working class people, free citizens or freed slaves with responsibilities and duties in trade, working for the government, etc.

Geographically they all appeared to be city dwellers. In Greco-Roman culture, any idea of importance was developed in the cities, ideas originating in the country were dismissed. It was a major accomplishment that Paul was able to take a small, agrarian faith from rural Galilee and establish it in cities within a few years after the death of Christ. The target market segment may not have come from any special neighborhood in the city.

The God-fearing Gentiles who listened to Paul believed in the monotheistic god of the Jews. They shared the same values and desires as the common urban dwellers, and they all existed in a harsh, cruel, and demanding society. Other religions were not very good at resolving the problems of urban living that resulted from overcrowding and filth that existed both inside apartments and out on the streets. Life was filled with death and illness, both physical and mental, as well as wounds suffered from work or from ill fate. There was no privacy or escape from life lived in the streets. The apartments were uncomfortable, small, dirty, and often unsafe – buildings regularly collapsed because of poor construction.

After Paul tentatively identified the God-fearing Gentiles as a target market segment, he made further evaluations:

1. He reviewed the segment again to determine if there were enough unique traits to distinguish it as a specific segment.

2. He decided if the potential market segment was of an adequate size to provide a meaningful response to a campaign.

3. He determined if the identified market segment was accessible and would respond to the message.

4. He decided how the success of a missionary journey or marketing campaign would be determined.

5. He determined how the faith of the Jesus Movement could answer the needs, wants and values of the target market segment.

If the responses to these points were favorable, then Paul should consider choosing this market segment as the target market for his campaign. Just as Paul sorted out a target market segment, you should research the area where you want to plant your church or develop your faith-based community. You need to ask these same questions of your intended market.

Paul's target market segment had shared particulars. The God-fearing trait that distinguished the segment was a major specific detail. There were enough members of the segment to make a mission to them justifiable. Paul decided to target this segment and abandoned his original target of Jews.

The selected homogeneous market segment then became the target market. If you have done your research, you know what your target segment wants and how it will respond to your campaign. You've found a market segment that will provide a favorable response for your work and efforts.

QUESTIONS FOR DISCUSSION AND THOUGHT STARTERS

1. What are some of the factors you can use to sort total or mass market into a segment that you can work with?

2. What are some ways you can determine what non-churchgoers consider of value?

3. If you were looking at an inner city location for your church, how would you determine what would be a target market segment?

4. When should you have your research results?

5. When is it time to designate a target market?

6. What happens during the campaign if you realize your selected market segment is in error?

Step 3

Where Does Your Church Fit?

The title of this step is "Where Does Your Church Fit?" This step is something over which you have some control. While you do not have control over the external conditions we discussed, you are able to manage the external elements that will provide you with a positive and success-oriented marketing campaign. What you are going to do is create a *marketing mix* that will enable you to communicate with your target market. Paul created a marketing mix for his second missionary journey; his mix connected with the target market of God-fearing Gentiles. His Movement provided answers that people were seeking in their harsh and dangerous environments.

Let's step back and think about how your new church or Christian community will "fit" as it responds to the needs and wants of the non-churchgoers in the neighborhood you are approaching. To be realistic, let's think about this new church as a "product introduction" into the religious economy. To think of your church as a product in merchandizing terms is not to put down your plan to plant a church. It just helps to understand the problems you are up against in our marketing culture. A religious economy is the system by which a consumer allocates limited resources. Consumers have limited resources in money and time, and they want to spend their resources in a manner that will best satisfy wants and needs. Your church provides specific methods to fulfill a consumer's wants and needs – methods that are different than those offered by other churches.

You can think of the introduction of your new church in the same manner as you might consider the introduction of a new automobile into the automobile economy. Remember, you have done the research and identified your target market. In the same way that an automobile company wants to satisfy prospective car buyers with a new automobile, think about how you want non-churchgoers to perceive your church. You know your target market of non-churchgoers; how will they perceive your church in comparison to other churches? When you think about a market position, you're thinking about how you can make your product competitive.

Continuing with the automobile analogy, are you going to place your product at the high end of the auto economy to compete with the Cadillac or Mercedes? Maybe you will position your car at a lower end of the automobile economy to compete with less expensive cars. The automobile economy is an organized system that categorizes different automobiles in terms of price, use and performance, design, etc. Similarly, a religious economy is an organized system comprised of all the differing churches or Christian communities, categorized in terms of what they promise, the requirements and practices, etc. The non-churchgoers will form a perception of your product, just as car buyers do. They will evaluate and rate your church in terms of their own use, comparing with all other religions available.

In Step 2, you sorted and separated the broad general market into a target market segment that you believe will respond in a positive way to the message of your new church or Christian community. This next step is to develop a marketing mix that you control in order to reach your target market segments. There are four elements to the marketing mix – the four P's of marketing – and we will see how Paul developed these for his marketing campaign in the first century. The four P's are both interrelated and interdependent activities through which you, like Paul, will connect with the consumer to meet your objective of planting a church of a Christian community. To reiterate, the four P's of marketing include *product*, *place*, *promotion* and *price*.

In Paul's first missionary journey, he and Barnabas set out with no research on who, when, where, why, or how they would connect with a target market that would welcome their new faith. The lesson learned from Paul's first missionary journey is that you need research on the proposed target market. He assumed that his target market in the Antioch church and the believing communities in Judea were the synagogue Jews, who would welcome this new Jewish cult of the Redeemer.

The Diaspora Jews, having lived for centuries among Gentiles, were not interested in changing their faith for this new Jesus Movement; they were content with their beliefs and practices. The Jesus Movement with the promised Redeemer was just another cult of Judaism of which there were many. Granted, the Jesus Movement presented an afterlife with Christ as the long-awaited Redeemer, but not many were waiting for the fulfillment of the law with a Redeemer. Paul was Jewish, and going head-to-head with Judaism was extremely difficult. The consumer saw the new product as a "me, too" product without enough beneficial advantages to warrant leaving Judaism.

Now back in Antioch, he evaluated the target audience he did reach; the market segment that responded was the God-fearing Gentiles. He understood they wanted a monotheistic god, which was why they were worshiping with the Jews. But they were different from the Jews in that they did not want to become Jews in order to worship their monotheistic god. They were Gentiles with different values and wants. Paul understood he needed to define the product of the Jesus Movements so that Gentiles could join. Your new church also needs to respond to the values, wants and needs of the target market of non-churchgoers.

Paul started to develop a marketing mix for his campaign that would set the Jesus Movement apart from the closest competition, Judaism. He developed a mix of the four elements of the marketing mix so that the Jesus Movement would have a position separate from all others in the religious economy. Your target market segment, like Paul's, drives the contents of the marketing mix: the choice of product features, places of distribution, promotional actions and prices. The combination of these components builds relationships with consumers, but the mix must be flexible enough to change depending on conditions. The marketing mix is established and controlled by the marketing manager.

The first element of the four P's of the marketing mix is the ***product***. The marketing manager decides that constitutes the product; Paul was the marketing manager for his campaign, just as you are the marketing manager for yours. Your core product in church planting is "… through Jesus the forgiveness of sins is proclaimed to you." *[Acts 13:38]* In turn for your belief in Him, He will atone for and set you free from your sins, and He will make a place for you in eternal life.

This is the core element of the product or faith. The belief or church you are planting has a core element. And like Paul, the faith you are offering has more than just the core element. In addition to the core element, the faith offers a bundle of tangible and intangible benefits that promise to please consumers. These add-on benefits make up a total product in the consumer's mind.

In today's merchandising environment, we expect a total product from an airline. The airline offers a core product of flying passengers from point A to point B. But if that were the only product the airline offered, we would soon look for more features to go with the flight. We want and expect comfortable seats and cabin conditions. We expect employees to be courteous. We assume our baggage will arrive undamaged on the same plane we do. These extras help make the total product. A marketing manager can use additional benefits around the core product to entice more consumers.

You need to determine what additional benefits will supplement the core benefit of the church you are planting or the new Christian community you want to start. The enhancements help to position the product more favorably in the consumer's mind. The total product of the Jesus Movement was a sense of love for one another. It was vastly different from the Greco-Roman lifestyle of berating and humiliating anyone who may be in a lesser class or poorer state than you. The Movement held victory in life and death through Christian love. Roman culture preached that victory in life and death was the result of military and physical conquest for the empire.

Some of the additional benefits that made a total product for Paul were:

1. To know God and experience the life He offers.

2. Living a life of love and caring for one's neighbors.

3. God promises his followers He will care for them during this life and in the next with their worship of Jesus Christ.

4. Members are required to show love and acceptance of new members and to provide an inclusive family environment for members through the house-church. Dining together filled a two-fold purpose: One, it was a commemoration of the last supper and bound the members in faith. Two, dining together was a high honor in Greco-Roman society.

5. The house-church membership provided business and social connections. It supported professionals in commerce. Membership in the church with other craftsmen and tradesmen served in place of the costly memberships they maintained for themselves in trade associations.

6. The church membership spread the mantle of Christian love to include care for the sick and elderly. The membership also provided a "proper" funeral, which was very important in Greco Roman society. Church membership eliminated the need for individuals to join and pay annual dues to a funeral society in order to have a "proper" funeral.

In response to your research on the target market segment, you want to put together a total package of benefits in addition to the core benefit of your new church or Christian community. You have researched the needs and wants of the non-churchgoers. Maybe the total package of benefits will include companionship with other committed Christians who believe like you – that belonging to a group that thinks and feels like you do is pleasing. Membership offers the opportunity for you to share the burdens of another member who needs support and prayer in a difficult time. There is an opportunity to share with others through performing good works for the less fortunate. There is also the opportunity to have a spiritual experience through the services; worshiping together with song and companionship is very satisfying and helpful in many ways.

The second element of the four P's of the marketing mix is **place**, which you control as the marketing manager for your campaign. Like Paul you must consider place in your church planting. Place includes *where* you make contact with the consumer and *when* contact is made. In Paul's day, the way to reach the target market segment was to share information about the product verbally. The target must physically hear of your product, and that message must make an impression. Paul could select a busy square, a street corner, an academic academy, a lecture hall, or a stage. He could select anywhere the target market segment could hear him.

The task of reaching the ears or eyes of non-churchgoers today involves dozens of combinations you can utilize to gain the attention of an individual. *Place* today can be speaking on the street, speaking on a radio or TV broadcast, recording your message on a DVD, or posting it on a website. You can use any modern communication tool so long as you hit your target market segment. Put your message in a place where the market will readily receive it – you have to go where they are to meet them.

Paul never seemed to allow an opportunity to preach or teach escape him. He preached in prison, on the banks of a river, and in the meeting places of Athens and Corinth. He shared his message everywhere he could reach his target market.

Place has another dimension: time. Paul not only took the opportunity to share his faith in whatever physical place he found himself, he also took the opportunity to preach and teach the faith whenever there was an opportunity. Once, when he was in prison, an earthquake occurred in the middle of the night. The commander of the prison rushed to Paul and asked what he must do to be saved. Paul made time immediately to share his faith with the jailer. The jailer was converted, as was his whole household. Another time, he had planned one Sabbath morning to go to a riverbank and pray. But Lydia saw him and wanted to know about his faith. He took the time to talk with her, and she and her household were converted.

Maybe the best place you can reach your target market is by radio during "drive time." You can produce a commercial, or participate in a talk show that targets the same market segment you are trying to reach. Maybe you can write a blog targeting your market segment, or you could use YouTube or another internet messaging system. You might even do a 30-second TV commercial and run during television shows that target the market segment you want to reach. You are limited only by your imagination in finding both a physical place to reach the non-churchgoers and a time when the target market will be listening. Radio and TV can be expensive, which is why the research you performed is so necessary. You do not have the liberty of wasting money on the factor of **place**.

The third element of the four P's of the marketing mix is **promotion**, which includes all forms of marketing communications that are used to talk to the target market segment. Promotion can include anything from a conversation with another individual to pieces created for print, radio and television. It also includes activities to generate interest in the product – for example, sponsorship of programs or contests to highlight the product, sponsorship and naming rights to a neighborhood playground, getting placement of the product in a movie, organizing clubs, putting up a website for your church or Christian community, creating a blog for yourself or linking up with other appropriate blogs.

In Paul's world, communication occurred primarily by talking directly to the target market. The first members in a community would then pass the faith on by oral communication and testimony. Then, as now, personal testimony from someone you know is perhaps the best kind of promotion. Another extremely effective promotional technique was to conduct a public activity. Paul very effectively used public activities such as performing miracles like healing the sick and lame or by casting out demons and devils. He also used a miracle to blind an adversary on Cyprus at the start of the first journey (Acts 13). This healing was a direct confrontation with the evil spirits and demons. Miracles clearly showed the power of the God about whom Paul was preaching.

In addition to public speaking and miracles, Paul used his letters to individuals and churches to promote the faith. Letters maintained friendships, were reassuring and strengthening to the early churches and their members, and answered questions regarding points of the faith. They were often kept, reread or passed along to others.

Today you have a superabundance of electronic and print resources to promote your church or Christian community. You have an almost unlimited toolbox from which to pick and chose promotion instruments. Your only requirement is that the promotion is directed to and heard by your target market. Professional communicators know that making a difference and motivating the target market requires that the audience hear the message three or four times. The more often you come at your market with differing media and activities, the better off you are in getting the target interested. You want the eyes and ears of the market. But every product is different, and every target market segment is different, so be ready to modify or change your promotions if you discover something that will be more successful.

The consumer goes through several states before adopting a product. The consumer first thinks about the product in the *awareness* stage. The second stage is *interest*, when the consumer develops a curiosity on his own about the idea. Third is *evaluation,* when the consumer asks the question, "What's in it for me"? The fourth stage is a *trial application* of the idea on a small scale as he tries out the practice, techniques and conditions of the new faith. Finally, the *adoption* stage occurs when the target market segment finds the idea acceptable.

The fourth and last component of the four P's of marketing is the **price**. *Price* is something of value the consumer will exchange to possess the total product. It may be money, property or possessions. The price needs to be high enough to make the purchase or adoption of the faith meaningful to the consumer but not so high that it prevents adoption.

Paul had trouble in establishing a price for Gentiles to join The Way. The believing Jews who joined The Way argued over establishing a price. The target market Paul fixed on was the god-fearing Gentile who lived in the Greco-Roman world of the empire. A significant number of members of the Antioch Church who were former Jews believed a Gentile must first become a Jew before he could become a member of the Jesus Movement. To become a Jew, males had to undergo circumcision. Gentile males had two objections to circumcision: first, to alter the body was repulsive to Greeks; and second, circumcision for an adult male is very painful.

Paul belonged to the anti-circumcision argument, but those who favored the circumcision argument believed that a compromise could not be reached. To resolve the matter, the leaders of the Antioch Church referred the question to the Jerusalem Council. The Council's position would solve the question and both parties would be satisfied.

The Council heard the question about circumcision and dismissed it as too high a price to ask Gentiles to pay. Instead, the Council established four conditions for joining The Movement. They were:

1. To abstain from foods sacrificed to idols.

2. To abstain from blood.

3. To abstain from meat of strangled animals.

4. To abstain from sexual immorality.

These four conditions were significant, especially the first three. Church members could only eat meat prepared in the Jewish Kosher manner. Because of the difficulty of obtaining fresh meat, the diet of the common Gentile was vegetarian. What meat they had was most often obtained from public animal sacrifices to other idols and gods. After the sacrifice, the temple priests would distribute the meat without cost to those in the crowd. The animals were not bled out in the kosher manner, and some sacrificial animals were strangled. The fourth requirement of abstaining from sexual immorality was not further identified. It could have been an effort to keep the new converts from returning to their old gods. It could also prevent church members from fraternizing or returning to old habits they had abandoned, such as using sexual activities to worship their pagan gods.

The established price of a product changes over time. You, as the marketing manager, determine a price you believe will lead non-churchgoers to accept that joining the faith is meaningful. The price must be high enough to make joining an important step, yet not so high that the prospective believer will refuse to pay.

Paul positioned the Jesus Movement to appeal to the god-fearing Gentiles who believed in a monotheistic God. He set it apart from Judaism – the other religion of the day with a monotheistic god – by the benefits achieved by members through activities of the home-church. He took The Movement to the major cities of the eastern part of the empire, and made himself available to potential believers day or night. He promoted the belief through preaching and teaching, performing miracles, and writing letters to individuals and churches. He set The Movement totally apart from Judaism by not requiring circumcision. The Movement taught that peace was obtained through love, and that God would care for the believer in exchange for the worship. Finally, Paul's Movement provided a relief for the urban dweller from the harsh and grim circumstances of the lifestyle of the day.

Paul based his choices for the marketing mix on his research. These components of product, place, promotion and price were flexible and could be mixed and matched depending on the circumstances of the day.

You can learn from Paul's experiences by updating the marketing mix for the 21st century. Your research will determine which target market segment will listen to your message. Research will also show you how to position your new church in the religious economy of the area. Your work to respond to the values of the non-churchgoers, taking your message to them any way you can, just as Paul did. They will not come to you unless they hear about you.

Develop a marketing mix to set it apart from the other churches, and to show how the new church responds to non-churchgoers' wants, needs and values.

This ends the research and planning phase of the strategic marketing campaign. You are now ready to develop your plan and show your backers how you are going to establish your new church or Christian community.

QUESTIONS FOR DISCUSSION AND THOUGHT STARTERS

1. Why does a marketing manager decide on a position for the product?

2. What are the four parts of the marketing mix the campaign manager controls?

3. In the marketing mix, which of the four elements do you think is the most important and why?

4. Is a marketing mix constant throughout the campaign, or can managers monitor the campaign and change the mix in an effort to reach more potential consumers?

5. What are some of the ways the marketing manager can tell if the mix is working?

6. Who do you think ultimately sets the price? Is it the seller or the buyer?

Step 4

Write That Successful Business Plan

Paul showed us how he looked for opportunities in his church planting efforts. The steps he took are steps we can take today. He began with a first missionary journey that served as a research campaign. Through his research he established that there was a market for his message called The Way, which later became known as the Jesus Movement. With his research results, he analyzed the other religions in the religious economy. He identified a target market segment of God-fearing Gentiles. An additional evaluation of the research enabled him to decide where to position the faith or product to ensure the best reception. In the very crowded religious marketplace of the first century CE, he established a unique organization of the house-church that distinguished The Way from all others in the minds of potential believers.

Would it be a "cheap" faith, easy to come by and easy to practice? Would the faith be too hard to join? Would it satisfy the believer's needs, or was it just like others out there competing for members?

The first three planning steps Paul completed included looking for opportunities for his product or faith, confirming there was a potential market large enough to justify a missionary journey or marketing campaign, and determining where to position the faith in the mind of the believer so that it was a unique and separate belief from all the others in the religious marketplace.

There was one more planning step for the campaign Paul needed to complete: writing a *successful business plan*. It has the same purpose as a blueprint for a building contractor. The plan lays out a direction for the company, describing the business operations and setting goals and objectives. It tells how the company intends to achieve goals and objectives, and projects the expected results. Moreover, it serves as the measure for evaluating each part of the business.

In short, it is a written description of what is intended so that potential backers, as well as employees, know what is expected and hoped for.

A successful business plan should clearly identify the nature of the operation and the requirements for personnel, materials, and financial resources. Within the business plan are separate components, including a management plan, a situational analysis, a marketing plan, a discussion of finances, and control procedures for operation of the business. Some of the basic concerns about a new campaign that a successful business plan addresses include:

1. What are the human resources needs and how will they be managed? Who will operate or manage the company? What is the management plan?

2. How will the company be organized?

3. How much capital is needed? What is the source of capital? What is the expected cash flow? How will accounting records be maintained?

4. How will performance be evaluated? What performance forecasts can be made?

5. Is everything legal and are licenses and permits secured?

   Like Paul's successful business, yours should include the following:

   • Executive Summary

   • Situation Analysis

   • Marketing Plan

   • Financials

   • Control Procedures

I. Executive Summary

The Executive Summary should explain in brief the key features of the plan. It is an overview that provides highlights or major points of the missionary journey or marketing campaign.

It should describe the organization's goals, status, its product, the benefits consumers will experience, and basic financial forecasts. All of the significant components of the plan should be listed.

II. Situation Analysis

A situation analysis interprets environmental conditions and possible changes. The analysis considers the organization's ability to capitalize on opportunities. Both environmental scanning and environmental monitoring are done to forecast conditions and to predict possible environmental changes. This tracks such items as demographic changes, movements in sales, or temporary or long-term trends that may affect the company and campaign.

Paul evaluated four major internal conditions of his organization: strengths, weaknesses, opportunities, and threats. He needed to understand the environment at a full 360 degrees. He was looking for anything that would hinder or help the company and campaign. At the same time, Paul evaluated the company's microenvironment in terms of customers, competitors, company and collaborators. He considered marketing activities from a customer's perspective: Who the customers are, what they will buy, and what the product means to the customer. In addition, the competition was defined and its strengths and weaknesses were examined.

This analysis should provide a description of the company or church organization and its operating requirements. It details the company's start-up needs, including where the needs can be filled, how much and when money is needed, and a projected cash flow. It seeks to project financial needs over the growth and operation of the company.

Paul spelled out management and organizational details, such as: What are the backgrounds and training of the managers? How will the company be organized? What are the responsibilities of company personnel?

III. Marketing Plan

Within the successful business plan there is a formal marketing plan that contains the desired goals for the campaign. It specifies the direction for the company's marketing efforts. There are sections on marketing objectives, target markets, product positioning and the marketing mix. Strategies to follow are detailed and the best courses of action for certain future events are stated. The marketing plan may be altered or thrown out during the progress of the campaign, but a plan must be prepared as a starting point.

The marketing plan itemizes who is responsible for managing what activities and assigns duties and functions of the position. It provides a planned timetable of when certain activities should be accompanied. This section lists the strategic marketing objectives, the target markets, positioning of the product, and the marketing mix needed to obtain these items.

Objectives are set that are action-oriented, quantifiable and measurable. These objectives establish the level of performance that the organization intends to achieve.

You should include a general statement of strategies for each part of the marketing mix (product, place, promotion, and price).

IV. Financials

Your financials should address in detail all of the operational financial needs, including cash flow and any sources of additional venture capital.

V. Control Procedures

Managerial control is established to ensure everyone involved in the organization is aware of the planned activities and that activities are executed in an effective manner to achieve the planned results.

Written and published performance standards are developed by supervisors and workers to insure tasks are completed as planned and so that employees will know the standards they are expected to attain.

Investigations and evaluations by management are conducted to determine if tasks are   performed as required. The evaluation also tells supporters and backers of the company if the goals and objectives are attained.

Keys to a Successful Business Plan

- A successful business plan is practical.
- The plan should have provisions for continual reviews and course corrections.
- The plan establishes responsibilities and assigns tasks to people or departments with established milestones and deadlines.
- Successful business plans have realistic goals and measurable objectives.

An Example of a Possible Business Plan for Paul's Missionary Journeys

The Jesus Movement Company

Business and Marketing Plan
Headquarters at Antioch on the Orontes River, Syria
December 45 CE

I. EXECUTIVE SUMMARY

The Jesus Movement (TJM), as it has come to be known, began as a cult of Orthodox Judaism in Galilee and Judea. First, it was called "The Way." It is now a separate religious faith or movement centered on Jesus Christ. The Holy Spirit revealed to the elders at the Antioch Church that Paul was selected for special work to spread the message. He and Barnabas then left for a first missionary journey or marketing campaign that provided invaluable information and data. The original assumption that the Jews would embrace the Movement was not entirely false. However, a more receptive target market segment was found in the urban Gentiles who were seeking a monotheistic god.

This research journey determined there was a market for the Jesus Movement in the profuse religious economy of the Roman Empire. Gentiles who seek a monotheistic god can be isolated, approached and converted.

The practice of the religion will be through house-churches that separate the new converts from other religions. Paul will teach disciples, who will spread the message by teaching, preaching, counseling and assisting with converts and house-churches. The message is that God cares for those who worship Him. Eternal life is achieved through Jesus by living His commandments to love one another and love the neighbor as himself or herself.

A minimum of venture capital is required. The house-churches will support themselves and provide some support for the ongoing missionary or marketing campaign. Paul and his disciples will work for their keep. The faith will spread through testimony of believers, as well as by the fact that it is helpful to individuals in the harsh and cruel urban lifestyle of the day.

The first research journey will be followed by the main missionary campaign from Antioch westward through the Roman provinces to Corinth. After completion of the main campaign, Paul will make a report to the Jerusalem Council. He will then make a third missionary journey or marketing campaign for evaluation and control. He will visit established house churches, to further teach and preach the faith, to resolve questions of doctrine, and to strengthen the faithful and renew friendships.

II. SITUATIONAL ANALYSIS

The living conditions in Greco-Roman cities are harsh, unforgiving, dreadful and dangerous. Society is rigidly divided into categories with levels clearly divided and maintained. Everyone is a patron or client and the relationships enable the society to flourish. There is a place for everyone and everyone is in a place. Barnabas, acting as a patron, takes Paul as his client in Jerusalem when Paul returned from the wilderness. He continues as the patron by getting Paul to come to Antioch to work with the church. Barnabas was the leader of the first research journey. Paul refuses to allow Mark to go on a second journey. "They had such a sharp disagreement that they parted company, Barnabas took Mark and sailed for Cyprus." *[Acts 15:39]* Paul is no longer a client to Barnabas. He becomes a patron leading the second missionary journey with Silas as his client, and followed by the addition of Timothy as a client.

Neither the Roman civil government nor the many religious faiths are adept at solving urban problems. Cities are masses of common people living in overcrowded, squalid and unsafe housing. Life is that of misery, danger, fear, despair and disease. At least half the children die at birth or before age five. There is intense ethnic discord in cities from transitory and migrant individuals and various tribes. Crime flourishes, and the streets are dangerous day and night. Paul is aware of this environment and moves to anticipate and deal with the lack of stability by creating the house-churches for members. The house-church provides a haven and is very successful in dealing with the problems of urban life.

Paul evaluates his organization's strengths, weaknesses, opportunities, and threats. Strength comes from God's command for Paul to undertake this work. A weakness is a lack of precedent for such a missionary or marketing campaign. There also is a lack of trained personnel, and funding is uncertain. Opportunity comes in the form of the open and curious attitude towards new religions and Rome's lack of censuring local religions.

The analysis also explains the organization's microenvironment in terms of the 4C's: customers, competitors, the company, and collaborators. The customer is the target market segment. Paul positions the faith so that it is perceived by the customers or converts to be a way of living that provides love for all and respite from the harsh and cruel life of civil society. The convert receives security if he is a new immigrant, a family to care for the widow and orphan, a hospital and care facility for the sick or elderly, a trade society for craftsmen and laborers, and a burial society to give a proper funeral for the deceased.

God-fearing Gentiles believe in the unique nature of the monotheistic God and the promise from God that He will care for them individually in this life and in the next so long as they worship Him. Caring for the convert in this life and after death is special to the Jesus Movement. *Customers* will buy because no other faith offers a better "product."

Competitors consist of all the Greco-Roman faiths and mysteries, which are practiced. There are so many of them and they are so fragmented that there is no strength in any of them. The Imperial Religion of the Emperor is extremely well endowed and provides lavish temples and daily meat offerings to the gods that are in turn given to the people. The Emperor is the godhead. The Jews are competing with a monotheistic god but Judaism requires all males to be circumcised as a sign of their membership in the faith. This prevents the God-fearing Gentiles from joining. Many Jews consider the Jesus Movement as an apostasy to true Judaism, and they block the spread of the faith wherever they can.

The *company* is comprised of Paul and his disciples preaching, teaching and living the commandments of love. When a house-church is established, it becomes the company locally and represents the faith. *Collaborators* include any operations that help the company, but are not part of the company. They take care of the outsourced tasks better performed by professionals so that the company can stay focused on its goals and objectives.

Planting a church is different from selling potato chips or automobiles in that the product of faith is ontological and relates to the very existence of man. It involves eschatological concerns of final events in the history of humankind. It involves death, the ultimate destiny of humanity and the end of the world. Selling potato chips is concerned with an immediate satisfaction of hunger and asks nothing more.

A Chief Executive Officer is needed for command, control and establishment of the house-churches. This executive also insures the standardization of the messages, and the capability and technical expertise of the disciples assisting Paul. Paul controls finances with the emphasis that the local church be self-supporting, or that it has a wealthy patron who will care for the house-church after Paul moves on.

Financial needs are minimal at the outset in that only Paul and one companion will start the journey from Antioch. Paul then adds Timothy as a helper, and continues to add more helpers as time goes by. The Jerusalem Council asks Paul to take up a collection from the new churches and return that collection to Jerusalem for use by the Council.

Management is placed in the hands of Paul. He operates on his own and adds other personnel as needed. Disciples of Paul act on his instructions, developing and assisting house-churches, and staying with them as they solidify and grow. A disciple appointed by Paul handles accounting of funds.

Collaborators furnish transportation by land and sea as required and can be obtained locally. Supplies are few and the Jewish scriptures are available. There is no written body of knowledge about the movement and the Gospels do not appear for 30 or more years.

III. MARKETING PLAN

The goal, or what the plan is intended to achieve, is to preach the faith of Christ Crucified as the Jesus Movement in the eastern part of the empire and among the God-fearing Gentiles.

1. Strategies: One strategy is to preach, lead discussions and provide demonstrations showing the power of God to intervene in this life. A second strategy is to assure the converts that Jesus does not forget them in this world and that if they worship Him, He will never forsake them. A third strategy is to follow up with house-churches through return visits, visits by disciples, and writing letters to them responding to questions of the faith. A fourth strategy is the permission to develop modified or changed strategies in the event of changes in society or other portions of the market environment. Paul can develop and execute alternative courses of action to achieve objectives.

2. Target market: God-fearing Gentiles who believe in and seek a relationship with the monotheistic God.

3. Market position: One is to present the Jesus Movement separate and apart from the legalistic and ritualistic Orthodox Judaism with the requirement that all males are circumcised in order to enter into a relationship with God. A second position is that members live apart from other religions, cults and mysteries with their sacrifices and the imperial concept that peace is attained through victory over others.

4. The marketing mix to attain the objectives:

   a. Product: The religious belief that Jesus Christ is the long awaited Redeemer who shows believers will attain justice through love and in the next world by grace.

   b. Place: A seeker can obtain the faith wherever he physically is, and at whatever time is fitting and convenient. Believers, disciples or teachers must be ready at any time and any place, regardless of personal choice, to respond to a request to know the Lord.

   c. Promotion: The faith is promoted through public preaching, one-on-one counseling, and teaching. It is also demonstrated by miracles. Those who first convert in a community are encouraged to share their new belief with friends, relatives, and others whom they may encounter.

  d. Price: The Jerusalem Council fixed the price of membership in the faith:

    (1) To abstain from food offered to idols.

    (2) To abstain from meat of strangled animals.

    (3) To abstain from blood.

    (4) To abstain from sexual immorality.

    5. Management and marketing responsibilities: Paul is the Chief Executive Officer (CEO) and Chief Marketing Officer (CMO) of the movement. The Jerusalem Council established this authority.

    6. Marketing objectives: An objective is action-oriented. It is a statement of the level of performance that the organization intends to achieve. Objectives define results in measurable terms. One measurable objective may be to approach a stranger each day and interest him in the message of life through justice and love of the Lord Jesus Christ. A second measurable objective is to establish a house-church in the community to create a sense of belonging and a community of faithful. A third measurable objective may be to train disciples, teachers and leaders to witness the faith in the local community, and to serve as resources to the church when Paul moves on.

IV. FINANCIALS

The Antioch Church provides start-up funds and any venture capital needed. After house-churches are established in cities, they will contribute to furthering the campaign and the expense of the missionaries if possible. If support is not sufficient, Paul and his staff will support themselves by working.

    At the request of the Jerusalem Council, Paul will collect money from the house-churches to carry back to Jerusalem, where the Council will distribute the money to the needy of the faith.

V. CONTROL PROCEDURES

Control procedures and acceptable performance standards are incorporated in the marketing plan to ensure everyone knows what they are required to do.

Upon completion of the missionary campaign,   Paul will return to Jerusalem with the offering requested by the Council. He will make a report as to the success of the campaign that took him from Antioch through Asia and to Corinth before returning to Jerusalem.

Paul and his disciples then make a second campaign over the same route, touching the house-churches he founded on the previous campaign. This is a follow-up or inspection journey visiting   house-churches and communities. He will review questions of faith and practice with church members, or he will send disciples to visit churches in his name. He will correct the believers to return them to the faith and practices he originally spread.

He will use letters to instruct and encourage church members and will evaluate the strength of the faith and works in the churches by:

  a.   How new converts are included into the community;

  b.   How effective the church is as a substitute for professional associations of tradesmen, artisans and merchants;

  c.   How effectively the leaders and patrons of the community are working;

  d.   How effective the nursing care for the ill and dying is;

  e.   How effective the church is in caring for the dead and performing the funeral rites;

  f.   How effective the house-church is in living out the teachings of the faith to provide love and care for members, and extend love to neighbors.

QUESTIONS FOR DISCUSSION AND THOUGHT STARTERS

1.   What is the major purpose of a business plan?

2.   How many parts are there to a business plan and what are they?

3.   Must the target market segment be clearly identified?

4.   What is a characteristic of a goal for a marketing campaign?

5.   What must be established in order to judge an objective for a marketing campaign?

6.   Can business and marketing plans be changed in the course of their execution?

Step 5

Work the Plan

You did your research and wrote your plan. Now is the time to put the plan to work. This is sometimes the hardest part. Managers who are new or not sure of themselves may want to go on tweaking points to get it just right, but no one knows if the plan is right until you put it into practice. You have to go out into the territory, meet the target market segment, show the product and "ask for the sale." This is the result of all the research and planning.

Did Paul know his plan would be so successful? He probably did because he had faith in his mission, but the proof is in the action. Will it work? He really doesn't know until he put it into action. Your plan, like Paul's plan, is based on the best information and research available, but you don't know if it will work until you put it into action.

You did the research like Paul to determine if there is opportunity for you to succeed with your product or brand of faith in the religious economy. You find there is an opportunity for the faith available for you. Then like Paul, you select a target market segment that is likely to be positive, and you direct your message to it. Maybe they are all from the same neighborhood of a city, or from a suburb. Perhaps they are all young married families with children and are about the same general age. They may have the same level of education or work in similar technical and specialty fields.

Paul determined his target market segment was the God-fearing Gentiles who believed in the idea of a monotheistic god. Otherwise, they were all hard-working people who were seeking relief from their harsh and bleak daily lives. Most of these people worshiped in Jewish synagogues, because Jews also believed in a monotheistic god. But the Gentiles could not become full Jews without the rite of circumcision for the men.

Working the plan requires a skilled manager. Research must be evaluated and plans prepared to create a written description of what will be done. Implementing the plan requires active skills of organizing and coordinating people, activities, and resources. Many actions will need attention, often at the same time. For example, one action will be the hiring of a support staff and ensuring the systems and activities of all departments work together. Another action is the hiring of sales or company representatives and also designing the training for them. Paul's missionary journey was essentially a marketing campaign based on acquiring new believers. If the sales representatives, missionaries or disciples did not get out of the office to put the plan in action, all efforts were wasted. For today's market, the requirements are the same. It is one thing to do the research, draw the conclusions, and write the plan with the marketing mix that will achieve the best results. It is another thing to carry out the plan.

A LITTLE BACKGROUND ON PAUL

The CEO should be an action officer, taking charge and leading. If Paul was anything, he certainly was an alpha male. He came to Jerusalem approximately fifteen years before and was present at the stoning of Stephen. He got himself hired on as one of the temple police to hunt down Jerusalem Jews who were members of a cult called "The Way." He was very successful at this. He wanted to do more so he hatched a scheme that he presented to the high priest that would authorize him to travel to Damascus, at temple expense, to hunt for cult members. He had the legal right to arrest any Jews who belonged to The Way and bring them back to Jerusalem as prisoners.

On his way to Damascus, Paul converted and then went into the desert for some time to think. He eventually made his way back to Jerusalem and went about in the city making an annoyance of himself by praising and preaching Jesus. Barnabas befriended him, and the Jerusalem Council took him in to get him off the streets because they did not want bad publicity. But Paul continued to be so outspoken that the Council decided he was drawing the wrong kind of attention. They paid him to get out of town and sail back to Tarsus.

Sometime later, the Council sent Barnabas to Antioch to bring some order to The Movement there. When he arrived, Barnabas realized the scene was too much for him to fix. He needed the personality of a man like Paul to help him bring some harmony and structure to the Antioch church.

Try to match up your skills with Paul's skills. You can be the most sincere and devout missionary; Paul was this and much more. But the missionary journey or marketing campaign will take on the "personality" you give to it.

Paul was a take-charge man who demonstrated he could do research and planning. In addition, he could organize people and get things done. His attitude towards the missionary campaign would be reflected in the attitude and spirit of his workers. With all the challenges on a missionary trip that had to be overcome, a passive leader would not have succeeded. In your own campaign to plant churches or develop Christian communities, you need to believe in yourself, make decisions and take charge. You will be ahead in the program and the rest of your team will reflect your attitude.

The first missionary campaign with Barnabas did not work out as planned. The men anticipated they could go into synagogues and by telling of Jesus as the long awaited Redeemer, they would convert Jews to The Way. This is called the "injection" method of creating awareness, acceptance and understanding. The theory was that all you had to do was shoot the target market with information and through reason; they would understand the superiority of your program. But spreading the message this way in the synagogues did not work with the Jews.

Paul and Barnabas were hounded and followed by synagogue Jews from Pisidian, Antioch through Iconium and Lystra. In Lystra, Paul was beaten and left for dead. However, he and Barnabas managed to go on to Derbe, where they decided to return through the cities they had visited. Acts tells they strengthened the brethren, and appointed elders for each of the house-churches.

The first campaign was a success, even though they were rejected by the synagogue Jews. It was a success in that it provided Paul and Barnabas with much-needed research as to just who could be a target audience. The first short campaign also determined there was an opportunity for the Jesus Movement to have a place among all the other religions, cults and mysteries in the Greco-Roman world. The journey allowed Paul to determine just how he wanted to present the faith so that converts would view The Way as separate from all the other faiths in the crowded religious marketplace of the first century.

At the time of the second missionary journey, Paul was much better organized and understood the audience and lifestyles of the communities where he would visit. This second missionary campaign is the important one where he went out to plant churches and faith communities. By looking at how Paul did it, you can adapt your plan for success.

When it was time to kick off the plan, Paul and Barnabas had a fight that resulted in the total breakup of the two. The fight was not about doctrine, or any of the materials such as the four P's of marketing. Strangely enough, it was over personnel. Barnabas wanted to take John Mark, who had been on the first journey and had left them after they finished on Cyprus. Paul refused to allow John Mark to go. So, Barnabas took Mark and set off for Cyprus, leaving Paul in Antioch.

Paul then took Silas as his companion. He was possibly the same Silas the Jerusalem Council sent down to Antioch to deliver their decision on membership requirements. Some sources say that Silas decided to remain in Antioch. Perhaps he helped in putting the final plan together and knew all the details. It certainly is to Paul's advantage to take him on the campaign because the Jerusalem Council trusted Silas and would believe the reports he made about Paul and the journey.

It was Spring 46 CE when Paul and Silas left Antioch. When they reached Lystra, they stopped to take an assessment of the journey. They had walked over 200 miles from Antioch, covering between 15 and 20 miles per day. *[Meeks, p. 18].* They were 10 days to two weeks into the journey and settled in a routine. But Paul now knew they needed another helper, someone young and strong, and with the freedom he had as the leader, he recruited Timothy as a helper and disciple.

On the second missionary journey perhaps some five years later, Paul met Timothy in Lystra where his mother was a member of the church. Church members in Iconium and Lystra vouched for Timothy, and Paul wanted to take him along on the rest of the journey. Timothy badly wanted to go to and submitted to circumcision as requested by Paul.

This second missionary journey began when Paul left Antioch in about April 46 CE. He traveled as far west as Corinth and remained there for a few years with Aquila and Priscilla. After being on the road for about five years, he returned to Jerusalem in the fall of 51 and brought with him the collection for the poor that the Council had requested. He then returned to Antioch to rest and recuperate.

PUTTING THE MARKETING MIX INTO PRACTICE

Throughout the second missionary journey, Paul put the marketing mix into practice, using combinations of the plan's parts based on the situational needs. The business and marketing plan Paul went to so much trouble to develop finally paid off. He, Silas and Timothy worked the four P's of marketing: product, place, promotion and price.

Product: The *core product* they were teaching was eternal life through accepting Jesus Christ as the Redeemer. There also were ancillary products that supplemented and added to the core product. The new services and beliefs would produce a unique and superior product in the mind of the consumer.

The total belief package brought a new culture of caring for others – not only for brothers in the faith but also for neighbors who need help. The religion taught "peace through justice" as opposed to the state religion of "peace through victory." Stark writes, "…once Christianity did appear, its superior capacity for meeting…chronic problems soon became evident and played a major role in its ultimate triumph." *[Stark, p. 162]* Paul taught that God cares for his followers here and now, and will be with them throughout life and in the hereafter.

a.   A primary added value was that God will not forget His followers.   It was a new concept to Greco-Roman religions and cults where there was no promise that God cares for the worshiper.   In the pagan cults and mysteries, the worshipers made sacrifices to the god in hopes of response to the supplications.

b.   A secondary added value was the house-church.   It was a form for the religion to provide a sense of community and place for the individual in a culture that required everyone to have a "place" and for everyone to be "in his place."   Belonging to a house-church was an intimate, shared and emotional experience during a life that often was harsh and cruel.   The common meal, celebrating the "last supper," also provided the intimate relationship of dining together, a distinctive and conspicuous practice in Greco-Roman society.   Belonging to a house-church required shunning involvement in another cult and avoidance of all other rituals.   For the newcomer to the city, the house-church gave an immediate sense of community and belonging to the outsider who may have been homesick, lost and disoriented.   Greco-Roman society abounded and bristled on confrontations between "better ones" and "lesser ones."   A constant game at all levels of society from the aristocracy to the slaves was the put-down, the belittlement, the picking on individuals perceived as being in lesser positions or status.   The faith was asking for a change to this lifestyle.

c.   A third added value was the Christian mantle of love of neighbor and random acts of mercy in assisting and caring for others who may be distressed, sick, hungry or dying.   This concept of love and caring for the homeless and sick was a new and much-needed service in Greco-Roman society where illnesses were frequent and usually fatal.   Knowing that a brother or sister would care for you was a relief.   Another important service was that brothers and sisters would provide the deceased member a proper funeral, which was so necessary at all levels of society.   The house-church took the place of the Roman burial societies indigenous to cities in the empire that provided "proper" funerals for members. Burial societies held annual meetings and elected each other to leadership positions with grand titles that added a sense of status and character to otherwise harsh lives. Societies collected dues as advance payments for a member's funeral.

d. A fourth added value was mutual support for artisans, craftsmen, tradesmen and manufacturers. The house-church community took the place of workers' societies for tradesmen and manufacturers. Membership also encouraged mutual support for businesses.

Place: Place or point of distribution required The Movement member to be ready to share the message of faith anywhere and anytime the opportunity presented itself. Places to proclaim the message may have been the streets, public squares, water fountains, or wherever people gathered. Paul demonstrated the use of place by talking to Lydia when they met on a riverbank on a Sabbath morning. He also demonstrated the willingness to provide the message to his distraught jailer in the middle of the night after a ruinous earthquake.

Promotion: Promotion was the means and way marketers directly presented the message to potential customers or converts. The primary means of promotion was the direct one-on-one conversation between a believer and a potential believer. Paul's travels provided him and his disciples with unlimited opportunities to talk with people, make cultural contacts, and establish networks of interpersonal relationships based on kinship, friendship and commerce.

As a public speaker Paul was, at best, a minor player in a large league. He had no political cache. He had no obvious social stature or ready access to the authorities. No one employed him to address public assemblies on state policy or public morals. Luke occasionally put him in front of Gentile crowds, but an artisan such as Paul would most likely have had little access to such public meetings — except when a crown was stirred up to lynch him. *[Griffith-Jones, p. 178]*

Paul wrote to the Thessalonians during the second missionary journey. This was the oldest Pauline letter we have:

"We had previously suffered and been insulted in Philippi, as you know, but with the help of our God, we dared to tell you his gospel in spite of strong opposition. For the appeal we make does not spring from error or impure motives, nor are we trying to trick you. On the contrary, we speak as men approved by God to be entrusted with the gospel. We are not trying to please men but God, who tests our hearts. You know we never used flattery, nor did we put on a mask to cover up greed—God is our witness. We were not looking for praise from men, not from you or anyone else." *[First Thess. 2:2-6]*

a. A second method of promotion was through testimony by an early adapter. The consumers who originally heard the message from Paul, Silas or Timothy and converted were the "first try-ers" or first adapters. If they were pleased with the product, they would tell friends who became "early adapters." These two groups probably knew each other personally and trusted each other. The personal relationships greatly enhanced the credibility of the message because they were hearing an endorsement from someone they trusted. The testimonial from a well-known source may be the oldest form of promotion and is as effective today as it was in the first century.

b. Another method of promotion was the miracle. The stories of Paul's miracles are vivid and demonstrate the power of God to intervene in life as we know it. Pagan religions claimed miracles. They were an expected and accepted method of promotion and gave proof of the god for all religions in the first century. If the prophet or apostle could not perform miracles, then his faith was not valid or powerful. Paul didn't need to touch a person for a miracle to occur. "God did extraordinary miracles without Paul, so that even handkerchiefs and aprons that had touched him were taken to the sick and their illnesses were cured and the evil spirits left them." *[Acts 19: 11-12]*

Price: There is always a price to obtain the product. There is always something of value to exchange for the product. For a Gentile to become a member of the Jesus Movement, members who had been Jews claimed that price was to become a Jew through circumcision of males. Early converts to the Jesus Movement were circumcised Jews. They then converted to the Jesus Movement. Paul believed circumcision was not necessary and argued as such, but neither side would yield. The elders of the Antioch Church knew this issue could not be settled in Antioch, so they sent Paul, Barnabas, and some others to Jerusalem to seek a resolution on price from the Jerusalem Council. The Council deliberated and responded with four requirements that were the price for membership.

Price, however, is elastic and flexible, and later in the third missionary Paul relaxed the rule.

"Eat anything sold in the meat market without raising questions of conscience, for, 'The earth is the Lord's, and everything in it.' If some unbeliever invites you to a meal and you want to go, eat whatever is put before you without raising questions of conscience. But if anyone says to you, 'This has been offered in sacrifice,' then do not eat it, both for the sake of the man who told you and for conscience' sake---the other man's conscience, I mean,

not yours. For why should my freedom be judged by another's conscience?"
[1 Cor. 10:25-30]

a. The first requirement is *to abstain from meat offered to idols.* To the urban
    dweller, this was a heavy price. Almost the only place for a common
    urban dweller to get meat for the diet was from that given freely to citizens
    after public sacrifices to the pagan gods. The temple priests distributed
    the excess fresh meat to people waiting for the handout. The usual daily
    diet was vegetarian because grain was easy to store and transport. Meat
    and fish were difficult to obtain and expensive because of the problems of
    storage and spoilage.

b. A second requirement to the price was to *avoid meat from strangled
    animals.* This ruled out animals not slaughtered in the kosher manner
    according to Jewish law. The Jewish method was to sever the neck and
    hang the animal so the blood would drain.

c. A third requirement to the price was *to abstain from blood.* The meat
    must be slaughtered in the kosher manner. "And wherever you live, you
    must not eat the blood of any bird or animal." *[Lev. 2:26]*

d. The fourth requirement to price was a prohibition that continues to
    cause confusion and divisiveness today: *to abstain from sexual immorality.*
    The three dietary restrictions are long forgotten but this restriction hangs
    on. The sexual debauchery of civil society, especially in Corinth, was
    beyond the norms, limits or imagination of today's society. The lifestyles
    in Corinth were even beyond the accepted standard of the day. The
    Greek language had an expression, "to Corinth," which meant to live
    in an extremely loose and licentious manner. Epicurean philosophy, a
    major philosophy of the time, held that all pleasures of the body were
    acceptable. Pleasures of the body were a reward for lives filled with
    illness, pain and death. Sexual activity for pleasure involved not only
    relationships between men and women, but activity with animals, male
    and female adults, and male and female children, heterosexual as well as
    homosexual.

This, carnal, erotic and gross conduct was patently offensive to the Jews
who were, by any standard, prudish, chaste and self-denying. Men and
women avoided nudity. Male Jews in Greco-Roman cities were modest to
the extent that they did not go to the baths. Neither did Jewish men exercise
in the nude, as the Greeks and Romans did.

Price went beyond these four rules, and additional costs developed for
the members. Suffering for the faith was a price to pay. Persecution, death

and deprivation were also costs for believers. Possessions were shared among all, and members accepted confiscation of property. Membership separated the member from former friends and sometimes from their own families. These rules served to place a high value in joining and being a member of The Way.

These four elements – product, place, promotion, and price, put together as a marketing mix – were what Paul and his disciplines used to establish The Way as separate from Judaism, and from any pagan religion.

You have isolated the 4P's of marketing that apply to your faith and the characteristics of your target market. You developed your itinerary with the blueprint of what you think needs done and you are free to make adjustments in the mix based on the environment you meet.

Paul and his party entered a city and gained one or two converts who were looking for relief from the harsh, belittling and cruel daily life. These first believers in turn would convert others. Paul selected individuals, both male and female, to become patrons for a house-church, such as when Lydia established a house-church. We can believe that after a small group of converts was established as a house-church and they accept the message, Paul and his companions move on.

The Holy Spirit was with them. They traveled through Phrygia and Galatia, but the Holy Spirit kept them from going into Asia for some reason. When they got to the border of Mysia they tried to enter Bithynia, but the Spirit would not allow it. So they passed by Mysia and went to Troas.

Paul had no contact with Antioch or Jerusalem but chose his course as he went. The Holy Spirit guided him to Philippi, the leading city of Macedonia. It was there on a Sabbath morning that he and his party met Lydia and her companions from Thyatira, who asked to be baptized. Lydia then took Paul and his party back to her place, and she became the patron of the church in her house.

Acts tells of Paul performing a miracle on a slave girl, destroying her ability to tell the future and destroying her value for her owners. Paul and his party were convicted of advocating illegal customs. After they were jailed, an earthquake occurred and the distraught jailer came to Paul asking what he could do to be saved.

Paul and his disciples left Philippi and went on to Thessalonica and Berea, and then Paul went on to Athens. He spoke with Greek philosophers in Athens, converting a few, and then went on to Corinth.

There he met Aquila and Priscilla and stayed in the city for over a year. Finally, Paul and the brothers sailed to Syria; Paul then went on to Ephesus and promised to return to his followers.

Paul went back to Jerusalem, made a report, presented the collection he made for the Council for the poor, and returned to Antioch for the first time in over five years. The Jerusalem Council welcomed him back and tacitly approved the work he accomplished by accepting the offering.

QUESTIONS FOR DISCUSSION AND THOUGHT STARTERS

1. Paul is both the author of the business plan and the principal salesperson on the first marketing campaign. What might be wrong with using Paul as the planner and the lead marketing person?

2. What were the roles of Silas and Timothy in the campaign?

3. Was Paul at liberty to make changes in the plan as the campaign progressed?

4. Do intermediate managers today generally have full authority to make changes?

5. Do you think executing the plan for Paul was difficult, and if so, in what ways?

6. What are some of the reasons price, as part of the marketing mix, would be changed?

Step 6

Controlling the Campaign and Evaluating Results

There are a couple of rules for management that need to be remembered; they applied during Paul's time, just as they do today. The first rule is, "Work gets done correctly if the boss is checking." The second rule for management is, "If anything can go wrong, it will." Management needs to check all work and correct anything that goes wrong. Consequently, control procedures are the final part of the business plan.

You planned the campaign, you set the standards and you are the judge of the success of your church planting. Is your marketing mix producing the best possible results? Were contacts with potential converts completed or just reported? Do the performance results match with those expected from the territory? What are good and bad results of the work of the campaign?

Your church planting campaign needs your evaluation of the results. You can follow feedback channels during the course of the campaign, but these do not necessarily report the true picture. Review during the course of the campaign will correct many items. Correction of any unforeseen issues requires continual monitoring so that the plan does not get sidetracked.

A comprehensive review and appraisal of the total marketing operation is called a *marketing audit*. There are many ways to perform a marketing audit. Perhaps the best way is to hire an outside, neutral consulting firm that undertakes the audit based on mutually agreed-upon areas of examination. Another way is to use an audit team from your own company. But because these individuals are aware of your interests and goals, the results may be biased. Trying to perform the audit yourself will not work because there is no impartiality. Regardless of how the audit is conducted, it will be costly in terms of both money and time.

Any review or evaluation of an operation can be upsetting or disturbing those being evaluated. It may also be very difficult for you, as the individual in charge, to admit that there are problems. You developed the program and have a personal stake in the success. It is your plan and you do not want to fail. This was true for Paul, just as it is for you. No matter who does the audit, management can and sometimes does influence the outcome of the report.

A marketing audit, by a third-party consulting firm, by an internal team, or by you, needs to follow these general guidelines:

1. The audit should be methodical and follow an orderly sequence of evaluation steps.

2. It should be thorough and far-reaching and consider all factors affecting market performance. The audit should also try to identify real problems, as well as symptoms of problems.

3. The audit should be periodic and occur on a regular schedule rather than randomly, which can cause suspicion among the staff.

It is best for management and the individual/firm conducting the audit to discuss the parameters that management wants reviewed and arrive at a mutually agreed-upon checklist. The audit does not need to cover all the following items, but should include most:

1. The environment: What current demographic trends may affect current strategies? Are there lifestyle changes that have occurred since the plan was written? How are other competitors affecting your campaign?

2. The objectives: Objectives are measurable achievements and accomplishments. Do the objectives fit the goals of the company? Should they be retained or modified?

3. The Strategy: Do the strategies support and achieve the objectives of the campaign? Can the strategies be improved based on the company's strengths and weaknesses?

4. Pricing decisions: Are changes in pricing successful in gaining converts?

5. Distribution: Is distribution made at the right place and at the right time, and in the right quantity?

6. Promotion decisions: Should there be changes in the promotional mix?

7. Market information: Is the market research still valid and current?

8. Activities of staff: Does staff travel conform to planned schedules? Are they justified by plans, and are they cost effective?

9. <u>Trained staff</u>: Do employees perform as trained? Are there ways to improve performance through new or additional training?

10. <u>Management</u>: Is it committed to hearing the truth about the campaign, even if the findings do not coincide with what management wants?

COMMON RELATIONSHIPS AMONG PLANNING, EXECUTION, AND CONTROL

Planning, execution and control are closely related. Considerations of the marketing environment lead to formulation of the marketing plans. These plans are based on the research findings. The company must review the execution of the plan through investigation and evaluation to determine if the marketing plans are executed and work as planned. When the marketing plan is audited, there must be an impartial basis for judging the success of the plan. The audit will review the planned activities and possibly report on changes in the environment reflecting different ways to execute the plan.

Paul spent about six years on his marketing campaign from Antioch to Corinth. He needed to judge how successful his plan was, how well he anticipated the environments, and how well the plan was executed. Like Paul, it is time to go back over the journey, evaluate what happened, and take any corrective measures that are needed.

You've returned from your missionary journey of planting churches in the territory where you did your research. You're probably very proud of the results. How have these churches done now that they've been on their own for some time? You receive emails and calls from them, but how did the missionary journey really go? Was it a success or a waste of time and money? Have the churches forgotten your teachings, changed their names, and now listening to some other doctrine? This happened in the Galatia church and in the Corinthian churches, which Paul had to correct by letters and visits. You included a control and evaluation section in your business plan; now is the time to discover those results.

PAUL'S CONTROL AND EVALUATION JOURNEY

Paul set out on what Acts indicates as a third missionary journey. In reality, it was a review of what happened to his house-churches and the faithful followers he left in cities on his second missionary journey (or first marketing campaign). After Paul had spent approximately six years on the second journey, he returned to report to the Jerusalem Council, which welcomed him and the collection he brought. Paul then proceeded to Antioch for the winter of 51- 52 CE and prepared for a follow-up evaluation and control journey. This was the Control Procedures section of his business plan.

This time Paul performed a marketing audit of the campaign. It would have been best if a third party had carried out the audit, but lacking any third party or large internal staff, Paul performed it himself. He knew his review had to be methodical, with orderly steps, so that all phases were judged by the same standards. The audit needed to be thorough and far-reaching, considering all factors of the environment in which the house-churches and followers existed.

He applied the same standards of performance for all the house-churches, disciples, and followers. Following is a list of factors Paul should consider when making his evaluation:

1. The Environment: Were there differing demographic trends in the cities than there were five years ago? What were the effects of competitive religions on The Movement's house-churches?

2. The Objectives: Were the measurable objectives of meeting one or more possible converts each day achieved? Was a religious community or house-church planted in each city visited? Was the training of new teachers and leaders effective? What did the objective measures show?

3. The Strategies: There were four strategies in his marketing plan. One was to preach, teach and perform miracles. A second was to assure converts that Jesus would not abandon them if they continued to worship Him. The third was to revisit house-churches. And the fourth was the freedom granted by the Jerusalem Council to make changes in strategies on the spot as Paul saw fit.

4. Pricing Decisions: Was the original price of keeping the food laws and avoiding immorality still effective, or was this price considered too high? Were possible converts turning away?

5. Distribution Program: Were the disciples and teachers willing to go where the target market was, and were they willing to share the message at whatever time and place the opportunity presented itself?

6. Promotion decisions: Did the planned marketing mix promote the message successfully?

7. Market Information: Were the God-fearing Gentiles still the target market? Also, did the converts consider themselves a unique faith apart from other religions, cults and mysteries?

8. <u>Activities of staff</u>: Were small staffs in each city working with the house-church and converts?

9. <u>Trained staff</u>: Were all disciples and representatives of the faith trained to Paul's standards?

10. <u>Management</u>: Was management committed to hearing and accepting the findings?

Paul also needed to review the effectiveness of the marketing mix (the 4Ps of marketing) and evaluate each part to determine if all items were still relevant or if changes should be made based on changes in the environment and target markets:

Product: Was there any change in the product – the belief that Jesus is the Redeemer who will take care of his worshipers in this world and the next?

Place: The original plan was to provide the message at any place and any time that a potential believer asked about it.

Promotion: Were the promotion techniques of public speaking, individual counseling, teaching and performing miracles to show God's intervention into this world still valid?

Price: Were the four rules for membership still effective? Were any of the membership rules relaxed? Was the sexual purity cost still enforced?

At his first stop in Ephesus, Paul found that believers were not sure they received the Holy Spirit when they were baptized. In the six or seven years since Paul was in the area, others had come preaching and perhaps poaching on Paul's believers. Paul did not train the self-appointed apostles that came to his established churches. They were not preaching his true faith. They named the baptism they performed as "John's baptism." Paul corrected this by telling that John's baptism was one of repentance and they were to believe in the one coming after John who is Jesus.

"...Paul took the road though the interior and arrived at Ephesus. There he found some disciples and asked them, 'Did you receive the Holy Spirit when you believed?'

They answered, 'No, we have not even heard that there is a Holy Sprit.'

So Paul asked, 'Then what baptism did you receive?'

'John's baptism,' they replied.

Paul said, 'John's baptism was a baptism of repentance. He told the people to believe in the one coming after him, that is, in Jesus.' On hearing this, they were baptized into the name of the Lord Jesus.

When Paul placed his hands on them, the Holy Spirit came on them, and they spoke in tongues and prophesied. There were about twelve men in all." *[Acts 19:1 – 7]*

Murphy's Law applied here just as it does today: "If anything can go wrong, it will." A variation is, "Whatever can go wrong will go wrong, and at the worst possible time, in the worst possible way."

You can see what was happening to Paul's converts can happen to your converts. You planted a church or faith community and stayed with them long enough to believe they knew the body of faith you preached and taught. But now, since you have a house-church working, those pesky newcomers down the street want to slip in and steal away your folks. The newcomers will have a slightly different emphasis or practice. Maybe their faith does not require so much of the believer, or maybe it requires more from the believer than the practices you left behind and therefore must be more important and better. In Paul's case, the new preachers simply told Paul's converts that he didn't know what he was doing, and that they were bringing the correct message and ways.

Paul preached and taught for about two years while he was in Ephesus so that Jews and Greeks who lived in the province of Asia would become familiar with the message. He wrote letters of advice and comfort to the church in Philippi, as well as a personal letter to Philemon, who lived in Colossae. The letter to Philemon asked him to take back his domestic slave Onesimus because he had aided Paul in Ephesus.

His reputation as a healer grew in Ephesus. Handkerchiefs and aprons that he touched were taken to the sick, and their illnesses were cured and the evil spirits left them. He cast out spirits, and many who practiced sorcery burned their scrolls with magical instructions.

A disciple named Apollos, trained by Aquila and Prisca, came to Ephesus and told Paul that his followers in Corinth were straying from the true teaching. At the same time, Paul was having trouble with the Galatians, who were turning to newer Judaizer missionaries. When he was in Antioch the winter of 51-52, it appeared that he may have lost an argument with hardline Jews of the circumcision party, a question the Jerusalem Council had covered about five years before. These were the same arguments between the pro-circumcision party, and Paul's anti-circumcision position. Apparently the pro-circumcision party was hanging on and winning support, even though the Jerusalem Council had resolved the question of circumcision. These hardline conservatives were infiltrating the Galatians' assemblies and stressing that converts must live by the Mosaic Law that included circumcision. "Paul stands for God's grace and rescue by faith; they [the hard line new teachers] stand by contrast for the rigid observance of the Law." *[Griffith-Jones, p. 225]*

New teachers in Galatia were drawing converts away from Paul. They challenged Paul, saying that he did not have institutional standing. However,

Paul argued that he took his message from a direct revelation from God that he received in the desert. He wrote a letter to the Galatians to try to reconnect with those churches. Paul believed he "...was made an emissary directly by God; they [the Galatians] shall inherit the promise made to Abraham's offspring—directly from God. They shall then be under no human authority but Paul's own; no other teacher will have any hold over them." *[Griffith-Jones, p. 235]*

In Corinth in the spring of 54, where the core of his followers were rich and powerful citizens, the bad news continued. *[Griffith-Jones, p. 274]* He sent Timothy to Corinth to get a full picture and to carry the letter we now know as First Corinthians. Paul did not think the situation was such that he needed to go personally.

Timothy took the letter to Corinth in the summer of 54 and returned to Paul in a few weeks to report that the situation has worsened. Paul knew he had a serious problem on his hands if he was to keep the Corinthians true to the belief he preached. He would have to make a personal visit to the churches. He sent Timothy and Erastus to Macedonia *[Acts 19:22]* in his place while he went directly to Corinth from Ephesus and then quickly returned. *["Note: The details of Paul's journeys to and from Corinth are famously hard to construct with confidence." Griffith-Jones, p. xi]* This is the painful visit he referred to in 2 Cor. 2:1 and 13:2.

Bad news continued to plague Paul from Corinth. After some time he finally went to Corinth and regained control of his churches. He was able to reach reconciliation between his teachings and the teachings of the later missionaries who taught a different doctrine. In Spring 56, he was ready to move on.

The message Paul initially put in place on the second journey should still be used. He steadfastly held that there was no change in the Jesus Movement, that it was same as it was when he first preached. Much of his time on the evaluation journey was spent correcting doctrine that had gone off-message and ensuring that his new apostles followed his doctrine and did not corrupt the churches he founded.

There was some relaxing of the price originally set for joining The Movement. He wrote to the Corinthians that the kosher dietary laws were not as strict as imagined. "Eat anything sold in the meat market without rising questions of conscience, for, 'The earth is the Lord's, and everything in it.'" *[1ˢᵗ Cor 10:25-26]* In his letter to the Romans, written when he is about to leave Corinth to return to Jerusalem, he did not mention any of the three original dietary laws: abstaining from meat sacrificed to idols, from meat of strangled animals, and from blood of meat not drained of blood as in the kosher manner.

Paul was satisfied with what he had done and was on his way to a new project. He wrote to the Romans, "But now that there is no more place for me to work in these regions, and since I have been longing for many years to see you, I plan to do so when I go to Spain..." *[Rom. 15:23-24]* He was ready to sail to Syria and then on to Jerusalem. But he learned of a plot against him, went overland back through Macedonia to avoid trouble, and then sailed from Philippi to Troas. He performed one last miracle in Troas. He spoke to a large crowd in a meeting room on a third floor. A young man named Eutychus was sitting on a windowsill and went to sleep. He fell out of the window and was believed dead. Paul immediately went down to the scene, put his arms around the young man, and Euthychus was revived. Friends took Euthychus home alive.

Paul met the elders at Miletus, exhorted them to keep the faith and hurried on to Jerusalem, which he wanted to reach by the day of Pentecost. He was welcomed in Jerusalem, where he reported to James and the elders on his accomplishments and the status of the faith during his journeys, which were ending.

Paul brought his marketing plan for the eastern cities of the empire to an end with this inspection, evaluation and corrective tour. He believed the faith as he preached it was safely established. He seemed satisfied with himself and was already planning another missionary campaign to another part of the empire. Let's hope the inspection trip you make to review your church planting effort is as positive as Paul's was. It seems that there were only minor problems here and there, and they were mostly from missionaries who wanted to hold to the law of circumcision. The sensible thing for Paul to do, since his health had apparently held up and he knew the best ways to plant churches, was to plan and make a follow-up missionary campaign to a new area where they had not heard of The Way or of Jesus the Redeemer.

QUESTIONS FOR DISCUSSION AND THOUGHT STARTERS

1. Do you think Paul was surprised that other missionaries were trying to poach from his followers in Corinth?

2. How does Paul make effective use of his helpers?

3. Do you think Paul was surprised by his findings on the inspection tour?

4. Do you think Paul was quick to seize on problem areas in the churches?

5. Why was Paul so concerned about the churches in Corinth?

6. Do you think Paul had any idea of what he might find in Jerusalem after all the time he was gone?

Step 7

Starting All Over Again

A marketing campaign is like a living thing. If it isn't going forward and growing, it's dying. It takes on a life of its own. Organizations are never static, never without movement. The churches you are planting, just as with the churches Paul planted, will either grow or decline. Paul's marketing campaigns – and hopefully yours – experienced initial success with the product, the Jesus Movement. But the organization wanted to keep on growing. The basic product of the Jesus Movement was a vital and living organization with the goal of growing where it was initially located and/or to reach out to new territories.

At this point, like Paul, you need to start planning for a new campaign. To do this, you must build on the original business plan and its marketing plan. The steps for a strategic campaign will be the same, only targeting a new territory. Paul had already settled on a new territory even before he left Corinth. He was proud of selecting Spain for his new campaign and he boasted of this in his letter to the Romans. Not only did he want to stop in Rome to reacquaint himself with old friends, but also he needed the financial support of the supposedly wealthy Roman churches. Paul was giving the Romans advance notice of the financial support and backing he needed.

He wrote:

"But now that there is no more place for me to work in these regions, and since I have been longing for many years to see you, I plan to do so when I go to Spain. I hope to visit you while passing through and to have you assist me on my journey there, after I have enjoyed your company for a while." *[Rom. 15:23-24]*

L. Michael White writes in *From Jesus to Christianity*: "In saying he wants 'to be sent on' to Spain by the house churches of Rome after 'enjoying your company' Paul was using the formal language of letters of recommendation. In other words, Paul was saying, 'I want you to show me hospitality and to pay for the next leg of my trip to Spain.' Undoubtedly some in Rome had heard of his troubles or considered him risky. Hence, by explaining his mission theology, the Roman letter was meant to lay the groundwork for them to be his new missionary patrons, just as the churches at Philippi had been in the Aegean." *[White, p. 210-211]*

There were various Jewish cults in the city, but the Jesus Movement made up of Gentiles was there for at least 10 years. The Roman historian Suetonius wrote that emperor Claudius expelled the Jews from Rome, probably in 49 CE, after repeated riots "instigated by Chreestus." *[Griffith-Jones. P.381]*

By the 60s CE, there were probably thirty to forty thousand Jews in Rome. We hear of different Roman prayer houses serving different Jews: those in the emperor's household; those connected with the government of Judea and Syria; those speaking Greek, those speaking Aramaic; those from southern Italy or from Africa. Some or all of the congregations would likely have met in the houses of wealthy members; there is still no clear evidence in first-century Rome of a purposely built prayer house or building converted to such use. "…Those followers of Jesus gravitated to the prayer houses whose own leaders shared their conviction and welcomed Christian teachers." *[Griffith – Jones, p. 382]*

Paul possibly knew there would be little financial support for the campaign to Spain from the Aegean part of the empire with its Greek-based culture and learning. The population in Spain was almost totally Gentile and, in addition to the local languages, Latin was the language of government and commerce. "There were few Jews in Spain and few Greek speakers; if [Paul] preached in Spain as he writes to Rome, he would have left his audience utterly confused." *[Griffith – Jones, p. 393]*

Paul did not know Spain and would need to develop and identify the strengths, weaknesses, opportunities and threats to his campaign organization. Rome was the center of the empire and he could conduct research there with sources familiar with Spain. There would be sailors, soldiers, traders, government officials and others who knew the country and could offer information, advice and counsel.

When you begin your campaign of planting churches or building Christian communities outside of the United States, you may experience some of the same conditions Paul confronted. If you are planting a church or mission in Brazil, you could experience a language barrier – Brazil's national language is Portuguese, and the customs will all be new to you. How will you raise interest in your church in a city versus a rural area? Perhaps you will do as so many others do – you will enter the territory providing a service such as medicine for the locals and then win them to your church.

If you are called to support a mission in Nigeria, it is very different. The language of Nigeria is English and it has its own long-held customs. The population is 50% is Muslim and 40% is Christian. The major Protestant denomination is the Anglican Church. You will have to do major research to understand and communicate with the people.

However, researching and developing the new marketing campaign is going to be much easier than the first campaign. You know how things work, so you will perform the same steps as you and Paul did for the first campaigns:

1. Investigate Opportunities: Perform a situational analysis of the territory as well as an environmental scan. Review your own organization and evaluate it for strengths, weaknesses, and opportunities and threats in the new territory. Based on the analysis, ask yourself if there is an opportunity for success with your church planting.

2. Determine Market Slices and Decide on a Target Slice: Can you identify a target market that will respond favorably? Identify who these persons are in the target market and how large it is. Does this target market offer big enough opportunities to warrant a campaign?

3. Determine a Market Position and Aim to Fill It: Where will you position your faith against all the other religions in the territory? How will your product compare to the competition? Carefully develop the marketing mix consisting of the 4Ps of marketing: Product, Place, Promotion and Price.

4. Write the Marketing Plan: You need the business plan to explain to others what you are going to do and how you will do it. It will serve as an outline or map for the campaign and as explanation to your potential backers what you plan to do. There will be five major sections, just as in the first campaign: executive summary, situational analysis, a marketing plan, financials, and control procedures.

5. Work the Plan: After you write the plan, use it. It is the base from which to start and your roadmap to success. You can't tell where you are going or where you are without a reference map. Use the 4Ps of marketing you established and change them as necessary. Ensure the *product* is presented as clearly as possible. Evaluate the concept of *place* so that the product is where it should be and at the appropriate time. Review *promotion* techniques for the target market. Finally, control the *price* so the product represents a quality item to the consumer and does not out-price itself.

6. Control Efforts and Evaluation Results; After you complete the mission, determine if the goals and measurable objectives of the campaign were achieved and how you can improve your results next time.

7. <u>Start All Over Again</u>: Review the lessons you learned from the completed campaign, and start over again, using the same steps for the new campaign.

PAUL STARTS OVER AGAIN

There can be nothing better for a marketing campaign than building a new campaign on a successful one. Paul was imminently successful in spreading the Jesus Movement from Antioch to Corinth. He took the peasant Jewish cult of the Jesus Movement out of rural Judea and the remote city of Jerusalem and transformed it to a dynamic urban religion that offered salvation after death, and more immediately, comfort, security and relief to the people living in the harsh and unforgiving Roman cities. The Jesus Movement enabled children and adults to find genuine friends who would aid each other. Believers bound themselves together in love for one another and love for Jesus Christ. The belief provided relief and knowledge that there was more to life than the Roman concept of peace through military victory. Paul's religion showed peace was attained through love, which was in direct opposition to the Roman imperial religion's mantra that peace was attained through victory over others. Living the Jesus Movement through the house-church communities showed a more flexible and caring lifestyle in comparison to typical harsh and unforgiving ways.

Paul preached that Jesus would care for the believer committed to Him. Paul took the Jesus Movement out of rural Judea and established it with the urban Gentiles. He transformed what was a minor Jewish peasant cult from the shore of the Sea of Galilee to a dynamic, life-giving and life-changing living religion that is still growing through faith.

He planned on getting financial support and backing from the Roman believers. Had he not been arrested in Jerusalem and had he not demanded a hearing before the Emperor, he would not have ended up in Rome as a prisoner waiting for a hearing before the Emperor. We can believe he would have been successful in his campaign again as he took the Movement to Spain.

Church planting is difficult in any circumstances. Introducing a new product into any market is difficult. This is probably especially true in Europe today where church attendance has fallen off so much. Here in the United States, Christianity is respected and an important aspect in the lives of a majority of citizens. Even with all the conveniences we have, it can still be difficult to spread the word. Think what it was like for Paul, a Pharisee Jew, moving about in a Greco-Roman lifestyle and combating hardships on all sides. He used concepts and techniques to help him spread the word of The Way. By reflecting on his methods, we can help our own church planting, even 2,000 years later.

QUESTIONS FOR DISCUSSION AND THOUGHT STARTERS

1. What were the advantages of Paul conducting the campaign to Spain rather than one of the other apostles doing it?

2. What are some of the specific things Paul can do to win over the Movement members in Rome to fund his campaign?

3. Some sources believe that Paul was not highly regarded in Rome. Could he have the reputation of a conceited, self-righteous man who did not take advice?

4. Paul had lived and worked in the Greco-Roman world of the eastern empire. Would he have to change some of his thinking to appeal to the western portion of the empire?

5. Do you think the rules for converts in Spain were the same as those for the first campaign?

6. Even though Paul did not go to Spain, but instead became a prisoner in Rome, do you think he was satisfied with the work he did for God in the Jesus Movement?

Appendix
Demons, Religions, and Cities

A demon is an evil spirit, devil, fiend, or an evil passion or influence. In the first century they were very real and active, and always present everywhere. No one questioned the reality of demons. There was no predicting what they would or would not do. Demons were considered the source of both good and bad fortune, responsible for both normal and paranormal events. Truth and fiction mixed in the Greco-Roman mind and things happened as the result of demons.

Demons were as pervasive and inescapable in the first century as germs are today. There was no scientific method to evaluate an event or determine the initiating cause or effect. Famines were considered the result of demonic activity, not of weather effects on crops. Efforts to calm, pacify, assuage and placate demons were carried out by priests, mystics, oracles, prophets and sacrifices to the gods. No Greek or Roman god promised to care for followers against demons.

Time and again, when Jesus or someone performed a miracle to aid or cure an individual, it was reported that the demons could be seen leaving the body. People sought relief from demonic forces. To a great extent, the effectiveness of a religion was judged by how it accommodated the demons. However, religions also had to respond to death, hardships, illnesses, hunger and cold. Greco-Roman gods never made specific promises to worshipers. Oracles made promises.

Hundreds of religions and cults practiced in society, presenting a nearly insurmountable barrier for a new product to penetrate. It was a full and mature marketplace filled with familiar cults, religions and practices. Perhaps the fact that there were so many cults and gods indicated that each one was weak individually, having little lasting effect on followers. The cults and deities required very little commitment or demands from followers. However, mystery cults of Isis, Osiris, Dionysus and Bacchus made promises and were very strong with believers. Individuals moved from one cult to another and could have more than one to believe in.

With the Jesus Movement, Paul introduced something new into the religious marketplace of cults, deities, mysteries, and oracles. The mystery cults were perhaps strongest among Greek pagan religions. However, the new religion of the Jesus Movement required abandonment of pagan religions and demanded full and lasting commitment from the believer. It required the convert to follow only Christ and reject all other gods. The belief also required the believer to make a lifestyle commitment and follow both love of others and love of God.

The new Jesus Movement faith demanded total commitment from the believer. In turn, God would care for the believer in this world and the next. The teachings and practices of the Jesus Movement were a new approach to life. Here, peace and love for a neighbor occurred through justice, which opposed the imperial religion that promised peace through victory over others. The Jesus Movement preached that following Jesus was a rewarding and satisfying way to live this life, and it promised a new life after death. The new faith was an effective response to daily life and to God.

CITIES OF THE FIRST CENTURY

The Roman provinces in Asia and Greece were peaceful and stable. Hundreds of years of successful governance of the provinces to the benefit of Rome continue uninterrupted. Royalty of conquered lands often continued to rule as client kings; friends of the emperor could rule a province. Professional administrators conducted the daily business of the provinces. A few of the administrators were slaves of the emperor, while others were free men.

Conquered cities were "Romanized" in three stages, with the first being construction of good roads and ports. Rodney Stark reports that because of the good roads:

"…anyone could cross the empire from one end to the other in a summer, and travel was common… Ronald Hoch estimates that Paul covered nearly 10 thousand miles on his missions…The people of the Roman Empire traveled more extensively and more easily than anyone before them did or would again until the nineteenth century." *[Stark, p. 135]* "…the bulk of trade and long-distance travel was by boat---Paul traveled as much or more by sea as by land…" *[Stark p. 136].*

The second stage of Romanizing a city occurred through the building of temples and the erection of statuary. This encouraged Greco-Roman religions and cults, as well as the imperial theology. The statues and carvings of heroic events constituted a public awareness campaign to remind everyone of the power and glory that was Rome.

The third stage in making a city a Roman city was the construction of aqueducts. The location of forts and cities was no longer limited by the accessibility of water. Clean, fresh and abundant water for drinking and cooking encouraged population growth and the development of an urban society. Abundant water enabled the flushing of sewer systems to help prevent diseases and epidemics. Additionally, the water supply supported public baths, which were a seductive luxury of the Roman lifestyle and a necessity in the hot Mediterranean climate.

The Romanizing process allowed local laws, customs, religions cults and traditions to continue so long as they did not challenge the empire. Habits, customs, and clothing in cities was different and varied. The Roman civic and military administration allowed for almost anything and everything except civil disobedience.

Paul lived and worked in Antioch for about 12 to 15 years before beginning his journeys. "Antioch, center of political, military and commercial communication between Rome and the Persian frontier and between Palestine and Asia Minor, was one of the three or four most important cities of the empire and the home of a large and vigorous Jewish Community." *[Meeks, p.10]*

All sorts of ideas came and went in Antioch, carried by merchants, traders, government and military visitors. Citizens had skills and jobs that helped keep the city running. There were construction workers, roofers, retail store clerks, bakers, restaurant cooks, city maintenance crews, and even travel agents. The latter arranged vacations for citizens with disposable time and money to visit mysterious Persia or fabled Alexandria, or to make pilgrimages to and from Jerusalem or Grecian "holy" sites.

Antioch had the supreme good fortune of "location." The city was on the east bank of the Orontes River, about 12 to 14 miles inland from the port of Seleucia Pieria. It was far enough inland that it experienced relief from the hot and humid seashore. It was also a welcome relief from the harsh and arid sun-bleached mountains to the north and east. Unfortunately, Antioch also sat on one or more active earthquake faults that destroyed the mud brick and wooden tenements over and over.

The city was well suited for the new cult of The Way, which later became known as the Jesus Movement. It was about 250 miles from Jerusalem, or a 12-14 day walking trip, considering 20 miles per day for the average traveler. Travelers could also sail between Jerusalem's port of Caesarea and Seleucia Pieria. Sailing was severely limited during the winter months due to contrary winds and rough seas.

"Any accurate portrait of Antioch in New Testament times must depict a city filled with misery, danger, fear, despair and hatred. A city where the average family lived a squalid life in filthy and cramped quarters, where at least half of the children died at birth or during infancy, and where most of the children who lived lost at least one parent before reaching maturity. A city filled with hatred and fears rooted in intense ethnic antagonisms and exacerbated by a constant stream of strangers. A city so lacking in a stable network of attachments that petty incidents could prompt mob violence. A city where crime flourished and the streets were dangerous at night. In addition, perhaps above all, a city repeatedly smashed by cataclysmic catastrophes: where a resident could expect literally to be homeless from time to time, providing that he or she be among the survivors.

"People living in such circumstances must often have despaired. Surely it would not be strange for them to have concluded that the end of days drew near. And surely too they must often have longed for relief, for hope, indeed for salvation." [Stark, p 160]

The imperial family, aristocracy, and wealthy in Rome and in the provincial cities lived in splendor; everyone else lived on a very modest scale.

"…large areas of Greco-Roman cities were occupied by public buildings. In Pompeii this area amounted to 35% of the city's area (Jashemski 1979), in Ostia [the seaport for Rome] 43% was taken up in this way (Meiggs 1974), and in Rome the public monumental sector occupied half of the city (Stambaugh 1988). If we assume that Antioch was average in this regard, we must subtract 40% of its area in order to calculate density." [Stark p. 150]

In 300 BCE, Alexander the Great, or one of his generals, established a fort that became the city. The original walls enclosed a little less than one square mile. Because it began as a fort, it was extremely costly and difficult to expand beyond the original walls. Over time, Antioch did expand outside the original walls and was about two miles long and one mile wide.

At the end of the 1st century there were about 150,000 people living within the walls. [Stark, pp. 150 ff] Life, as in any Greco-Roman city, was a public event. With a population of 150,000, there were about 75,000 persons per square mile, or 195 individuals per acre. This was less dense than Rome, which one estimate places at about 300 persons per acre. [Stark, p.149]

People gossiped, argued, transacted business and entertained each other in the streets and squares. Daily life was a social occasion of talking and touching. Private space was literally non-existent and all social levels mixed.

Most families lived in tiny one-room apartment cubicles. There was no running water, no toilet, and the window was a hole in the wall. Tenants heated the room and cooked with a charcoal brazier. There was no chimney to draw off smoke. Someone carried water in from the numerous fountains.

Everyone used public baths and toilets. With all of the activity night and day in one room, there was no privacy.

Apartments were always hot, cold, muggy, smoky, drafty, rank or foul. They were often dark because windows were covered by wooden shutters, cloth or leather curtains to help keep the room warm in winter; it also kept the smoke in and the light out. In hot weather, the room was cooled by wind blowing through an open window – which also allowed for insects to enter. The crowded living conditions bred vermin, rats, flies, and ticks. It never occurred to people that their living conditions encouraged diseases. Rather, people believed that demons caused disease; they were everywhere and inescapable.

It is doubtful that people could actually spend much time in such cramped and squalid quarters. The typical residents of Greco-Roman cities probably spent their lives mainly in public places, with the apartment serving primarily as a place to sleep and store possessions.

The tenements were about five or six stories high. The building codes in Rome limited apartment buildings to approximately 65.5 feet, or six stories. The construction technique consisted of weight-bearing mud brick walls with wooden floors. Buildings routinely collapsed from earthquakes or from dangerous and inappropriate use. Property owners divided and subdivided floors into more apartments to gain the highest income from the building. The smallest apartments and the majority of people resided on the upper floors. When these collapsed, they killed or maimed both tenants and passersby. There was constant danger of fire with no fire-fighting program.

Streets were narrow and foul. The density of the people and animals would place a heavy burden even on today's water and wastewater systems. Unpleasant odors penetrated tenements, public buildings and private homes.

There were no laundry soaps or detergents. Clothes were washed by trampling them in vats of human urine. There were no effective cleaners for floors, tiles, walls, or drains. The smell of a crowd at an outdoor event in the heat and sun of the Mediterranean climate was overwhelming.

Meals consisted mainly of vegetarian "takeout" from one of the many street level restaurants, bakeries, shops or street vendors. Problems from cooking over a brazier in an apartment made it more convenient to eat at a street level food shop, or buy a meal and take it back for the family to eat in the apartment, on the street, or in a public place. Grains, fruits and vegetables were food staples. Fresh meat was rare because of transportation and spoilage problems. The poor got their meat from the free public disposal of animals sacrificed daily at the many temples.

Activities began at sunrise to get work so that work could be finished before the hottest part of the day. Then from around 2 p.m. until sunset there was leisure time, which was often spent at the baths. Activities, work and travel were limited to sunlight by day and fires by night. Filling room with light or illuminating streets was virtually impossible. Entertainments, meetings and social gatherings all ended before dark. Travel in a city or through the country at night was difficult, dangerous and often impossible.

THE ROMAN PATRONAGE LIFESTYLE

Roman society was one of strict social classes clearly marked and well defined. There was a place for everyone, and everyone had a place. All of Roman society throughout the empire used an omnipresent and universal patronage system. It functioned at all levels – rich or poor, young or old, free or slave, in Rome or in the provinces. Everyone participated, from the emperor down to and including the lowest slaves. The practice was what made society work.

"It was patronage that kept the wheels of the Roman economy, society and politics turning." *[McManus, Barbara F., Roman Social Class and Public Display, The College of New Rochelle, July 2003, http://www.vroma. org/~bmcmanus/socia class.html, 4Feb2006 College of New Rochelle]*

There was also public patronage in which a patron became the protector or benefactor to a client group, such as a craft guild, a religious association, a sports team, or even an entire city. This patronage included gifts of money, entertainment, protection and advocacy.

The patronage lifestyle played a major role in the spread of the Jesus Movement. When a leader of a household, male or female, converted to the Jesus Movement, all family members, relatives, slaves and clients also converted. When a patron converted, it was expected his clients would also convert.

Barnabas became the patron to Paul when Paul first came to Jerusalem after his conversion and living in the desert. Paul was making a nuisance of himself, proclaiming the Jesus Movement to the extent that the brothers were afraid the authorities would begin to harass the small movement. Barnabas became his patron and took him on as a client, introduced him to the brothers, and tried to quiet him. However, Paul could not be controlled, so the brothers sent him home to Tarsus.

Later Barnabas was acting as patron when he went to Tarsus and brought Paul back to Antioch to help with the church. On the first missionary journey, Barnabas was the leader and patron. By the time Paul was ready to begin the second missionary journey, or first strategic marketing campaign, the two men had an irreconcilable argument over who would accompany them on the journey. Barnabas argued to take John Mark, but Paul refused since John Mark deserted them on the first journey. Barnabas set off on his own journey with John Mark. Paul, no longer a client to Barnabas, then became a patron and leader of a missionary journey. He took Silas as a client, companion, and helper on the trip. Later, Paul added Timothy as a client, relying on these two from then on while he completed the second and third journeys.

We may not understand the world of Paul with its mysteries and, to us, strange ways of doing things and thinking. But it was the most advanced civilization of the time, and it did function to protect the people and feed them. The Way preached victory through love of others, a philosophy different from the state method. The Way also preached that if the individual committed himself to God, then God would take care of him. Lastly, members of house-churches became a family, sharing problems and adverse conditions, and rejoicing in the good times of the members. They rejoiced in the love of God.